# OLDER PEOPLE
# AND THE CHURCH

© 2001 Trustees for Methodist Church Purposes

ISBN 1 85852 206 4

# CONTENTS

# INTRODUCTION

Why such concern about losing older people? Aren't the churches full of them? Should we not rather be concentrating on winning and keeping young people?

Yes, it is true that there is a preponderance of older people at least in the mainstream Christian denominations in Britain. In England the percentage of people over 65 amongst all church attenders has increased from 19% to 25% since 1989. In some denominations such as the Methodist and United Reformed Churches the figure is 38%. [1] However, such statistics serve to underline my concern that older people can often be short-changed by churches.

This came home to me quite powerfully when conducting a seminar with a group of new ministers who were continuing their training whilst already serving in churches. On enquiry none of their churches had formulated mission statements or strategies that gave any priority to the needs of older people, even though in several cases they were largely elderly congregations. One participant confessed to his shame that his church had only just agreed theirs and the entire emphasis was upon young people and families.

I subsequently received such a mission statement from a church where I had ministered more than 30 years before. It stated that they were an ageing congregation and drew the seemingly inevitable conclusion that every effort should be made to reach out to and retain younger people to correct the balance. No mention of seeking more effectively to meet the needs of the many older people they already had and who comprised such a high proportion of their local community! No affirmation of the positive contribution they made.

In no way am I maintaining that a concern for younger people should be anything other than a high priority. The recently published age profiles of the main denominations in this country [2] and the findings of the English Churches

1

Attendance Survey carried out by Christian Research in 1998 and published as *The Tide is Running Out* [3] should leave us in no doubt about that. The plain facts are that the Churches are collectively losing 1,000 children every week, and the number of young people up to 19 halved in the last two decades of the 20th century with an almost equivalent drop amongst those in their 20s. What I am pleading for, however, is that concern for older people should occupy an equal place in the planning and provision of the Churches, and of that I see as yet little sign. Woe betide us if we are so intent on providing for those we do not have in our churches that we neglect those we do have!

Part of the problem has been that the Jewish heritage within the Christian tradition has been obscured. It is evident from the Old Testament that older people were regarded as deserving special respect within the community of the people of God. It is even more evident in the Apocrypha, as witness the many references to its books in the 26 October 1999 'letter to the elderly' of Pope John Paul II. However, this is nowhere near as clear in the New Testament simply because it was taken for granted. Thus Paul's picture of Christians' unity in Christ in which there is no discrimination between Jews and Gentiles, slaves and free, men and women, does not mention old and young – because there was no need. Likewise Jesus, in his picture of the dividing of the sheep and the goats at the Last Judgement, mentions caring for the needy, the foreigner, the sick and those in prison with no reference to the old. It was taken for granted that older people were well cared for within the Jewish community.

However, had they lived today I feel sure that both Jesus and the Apostle would have explicitly singled out older people, and for good reason. Without doubt older people by and large are regarded as second-class citizens in our modern western society, even somewhat of a burden upon those still 'economically active'. After all, are not the over-65s soon to overtake in number the under-16s in our population? The media give the distinct impression that young is beautiful and being old is to be avoided at almost

2

any cost. It is currently fashionable to seek to deny the very process of ageing (together with death itself) let alone detect anything of value in it. Ageism is rife in employment and in many other spheres of life, including increasingly health services and social care.

Sometimes churches are accused of ageism in reverse, that is that they have become time capsules where older people can exert undue influence and dig their heels in against younger people and new ideas. There may be a measure of truth in this contention in some places but rather more often older people find themselves unaffirmed and to one degree or another marginalised in church communities. This simply compounds their problem.

Philip Richter and Leslie Francis, in their unique investigation of the haemorrhaging of church members, rightly comment:

> Old age, whilst it may bring poorer health and less mobility, gives people more spare time to be involved in the church. The awareness that human life does not go on forever can stimulate a renewed interest in the spiritual dimension. Old age presents the church with new opportunities, as well as challenging problems.[4]

In an ageist society what older people desperately need to hear and to experience is that ageing can be a positive process, that they have so much to give and to share, that they deserve credit for having kept the faith and held onto important values, that they have proved themselves to be effective 'friendship evangelists' amongst their contemporaries, and that, by the grace of God, the best is yet to be. In other words, they need to feel affirmed and valued. That every person is uniquely and eternally valued by God is surely at the very heart of the Christian Gospel.

When Andrew Cunnington arrived in his new Sussex parishes with the reputation of having a particular gift of working with young families, he was struck by the way his new parishioners apologised to him for their grey hairs.

Recognising the generally low profile of older people in churches, he subsequently spent a sabbatical in investigation and reflection and produced a booklet affirming their positive place and contribution.[5]

A few years ago I confess that I would have been amongst those who spare little thought for older Christians and feel that the Church's hope lies in its younger constituency. As I was working in school and university chaplaincies and in 'younger' churches, this was probably both inevitable and necessary. More recently, several years ministering in an elderly but highly active church and seven years working as Senior Chaplain with Methodist Homes have taught me a great deal. I am now a committed apostle in the cause of older people in churches. Hence my editing of this book. This most recent phase in my faith journey has also been a necessary and salutary preparation for my own old age as I face retirement in the near future! This book is therefore dedicated to those many older people from whom I have learned so much. I, with them and Robert Browning's Rabbi ben Ezra, dare to believe that in God's good providence 'the best is yet to be'.

The group responsible for producing this book has been networking together in the Sir Halley Stewart Age Awareness Project for the past six years and is a thoroughly ecumenical one. I have written the first chapter and acted as editor. Laraine Moffitt, who was responsible for chapter two, is a Roman Catholic. Chapter three was written by Gaynor Hammond, a Baptist, and Rev Jackie Treetops, an Anglican. 'Worshipping' is contributed by Raymond Clarke of the United Reformed Church and chapter five by Rev Jeffrey Harris, a Methodist. The final chapter comes from Heather Wraight, Assistant Director of Christian Research. I am deeply indebted to the whole team.

*Albert Jewell*
*Senior Chaplain*
*Methodist Homes*

**References**
1  Peter Brierley, *The Tide is Running Out*, Christian Research, 2000 p.117.
2  Peter Brierley, *UK Christian Handbook Religious Trends 2000/2001 No 2*, Christian Research, 2000.
3  *The Tide is Running Out* op. cit.
4  Philip Richter and Leslie Francis, *Gone but not Forgotten*, DLT, 1998 p.155.
5  Andrew Cunnington, *How Can This Be?*, Chichester Diocese, 2000.

# Chapter One

# BEGINNINGS

The origins of this book go back some years and I would regard the whole process as providential: God-guided.

Early in 1994 the *Methodist Recorder* published a series of five perceptive articles on ministry to the needs of older people by Rev Jeffrey Harris, sometime Secretary of the Home Mission Division of the Methodist Church who a few years previously had retired after 40 years of active ministry. Ministering at the time in churches that were predominantly elderly, I personally was so impressed that I cut them out and retain them to this day. It was Jeffrey who introduced me to Jung's concept of the process of 'individuation' or integration which can be seen as the main agenda of the second half of life. Jeffrey wrote from his own experience in retirement and reflected upon the lack of preparation of ministers in most denominations in Britain for ministry to older people.

I became Pastoral Director of Methodist Homes in the following September and soon heard from Jeffrey that the attention of the Cambridge-based Sir Halley Stewart Trust had been drawn to his articles and, although the Trust mainly focused on medical, scientific and social science projects, they wished to see something done to help address this neglected area. I submitted a proposal to network with other organisations, such as the secular Centre for Policy on Ageing, the ecumenical Christian Council on Ageing, and Faith in Elderly People Leeds which I knew was doing sterling work in raising the awareness of local churches to the spiritual needs of older people following Faith in the City and the ground-breaking Church of England 1990 report *Ageing.*[1] It should not have come as a surprise to me to find that a number of people in Leeds with whom I had worked ecumenically in rather different spheres years before when a minister in that area were now involved with this group – we had inevitably all grown older in the interim!

And so the Sir Halley Stewart Age Awareness Project was born. A bid was put in to the Trust to enable the production of two resources. The first was to be a booklet for local churches similar in size to those produced for ecumenical Lent groups, the second a training module for ministers. In the event much effort was expended by various fully ecumenical working groups and the resources were launched in the autumn of 1998. These comprised:

- a module for initial and in-service ministerial formation, *Spiritual Perspectives on Ageing*, of which some 700 have been distributed;[2]
- 10 booklets (rather than one) addressing a number of the spiritual needs of older people, sales of which soon necessitated the printing of an additional 1,000 sets;[3]
- a booklet by the Leeds group written by Rev Jackie Treetops, *Holy, Holy, Holy*, concerning the Church's ministry with people with dementia;[4]
- a more specialist and academic publication, *Spirituality and Ageing*.[5]

It was my privilege to act as editor for all these resources. The memorable keynote speaker at the launch of these resources in London was the Jesuit writer Father Gerard W Hughes whose subject was 'Recognising the Gift': the gift of an ever-maturing experience of God.

A total of more than 30 individuals from all church traditions formed the Halley Stewart network, many of whom have been subsequently involved in presentations to church groups and in training courses at various levels, directly or indirectly continuing the work of raising awareness of the spiritual needs of older people throughout the country. One of the 'knock-on effects' in which I am personally involved has been the establishment by Methodist Homes of a Centre for the Spirituality of Ageing at Leeds which is pioneering courses of various kinds and encouraging research.

The original intention of the Sir Halley Stewart Age Project was that it should be short-term, making an initial impact and producing low price resources which would ensure an ongoing effect rather like that of a pebble dropped into a pool; or, to change the metaphor, to give something of a kick-start to the process of raising awareness of the spiritual issues of ageing in the church constituency and the wider community. To change the metaphor yet again, the project has been successful insofar as there is now a quite exciting groundswell across the Churches of enthusiasts for the cause. Permeating church strategy, mission statements and activity may, however, take a little longer!

When the project planning group reconvened at the end of 1998 they recognised that there was one further piece of work they would like to accomplish. During the earlier work in which we were engaged we had each of us heard the anguished cries of some older people who for all kinds of reasons felt left out, neglected or marginalised by the Church. A woman in her 80s phoned up in distress that, although she had given many years of dedicated service to church and community, now that she was blind and frail they no longer seemed interested in her; fortunately she was able to move denomination to a more welcoming fellowship. Another who lived a few miles from the church she attended felt similarly following the loss of her husband who had been the car driver. A third wrote at considerable length, and on behalf of a number of fellow church members of a similar age, to say how they were only just managing to hang on to their church connection because Christian preachers and fellowship groups simply did not seem to want to know about the challenges to their faith that longstanding Christians faced, their need still to be nurtured in their spiritual growth and their deep desire for relevant and sustaining worship.

Without doubt there is considerable suffering and forbearance on the part of a disquieting number of older church members. Their voices are rarely raised in open complaint but they feel this neglect and insensitivity very deeply. We were convinced that much of this was due to ignorance and a lack of empathy with the situation and feelings of older church members as well as an unwillingness to divert precious church resources to such a large but 'unglamorous' section of the church family.

The final stage of the project was therefore established with the aims:

- To make the voices of disaffected older people heard
- To seek to analyse the various ways in which they feel marginalised
- To suggest what churches might do to address the situation.

The Sir Halley Stewart Trust willingly made a further grant available and this book is the humble outcome.

As a first step, and in order to test our hypothesis that there is a significant level of disaffection amongst older people who currently or had previously belonged to churches, we devised a rough pilot questionnaire (Appendix 2), 90 copies of which were distributed by those in the planning group. The sample was necessarily small and rather selective, most of those approached had lengthy church association and we did not reach many amongst those long isolated from the Christian community.    Forty-five responses were received, most expressing satisfaction that their spiritual and fellowship needs were being met. However, a significant minority were very articulate in expressing their disaffection.  The following four main areas of concern were identified:

- Worship
- 'Belonging'
- Loss of role
- The integrity and relevance of faith.

Such disaffection can be broadly summarised as perceiving a mismatch between what often appears to be the Church's agenda and real life insofar as older people are concerned.

We recognised that a more extensive and scientific research base was required if any outcome to our work was to have credibility. We therefore commissioned Christian Research to investigate further and agreed with them two complementary lines of approach, qualitative and quantitative. The first involved the use of 'focus groups' of older people, the second wide distribution of a questionnaire to existing church members with a further copy to be passed to another older person with no recent known church connection.

Six focus groups were held in different parts of the country to give a mixture of social contexts, gender, denomination and ages from 60 to 80 plus. A total of 59 persons attended (of whom 41 were women, 23 being still married) each having completed a short questionnaire in advance (Appendix 3). The meetings were carefully structured to enable the issues that the planning group had already detected to be raised but to be open to a wide range of views of the church (Appendix 4).

The full report and analysis made by Christian Research showed that on the whole current churchgoers attending the groups expressed satisfaction that their spiritual needs were being met. In some groups there were concentrations of people from the same church in which they were obviously well looked after, and it was difficult to judge whether the non-churchgoers felt free to be totally honest. In any case, where participants were able to identify such positive factors, as much can be learned from them as from expressions of disaffection.

Some of the main conclusions were as follows:

- Those who had stopped attending church at some time in the past (almost a third) had mostly done so for personal reasons (family responsibilities, work, removal etc), these being evenly spread over different periods in their life, rather than because of anything in the life of the church. On the other hand a good number of churchgoers continued to attend habitually despite admitting that 'church can be boring'!
- Amongst those continuing to attend, fellowship, friendship and spiritual support (especially in times of

bereavement) were the most important factors. The church's role in providing friendship activities and opportunities was obviously vital. Participants felt it is important to be known by name and to be accepted for who they are rather than just for what they can do. For the non-churchgoers 'cliquishness' and unfriendliness were the most significant turn-off factors and they chose to find their support elsewhere. All groups showed high membership of other non-church clubs and organisations, notably and somewhat incongruously the National Trust! They very largely comprised lively 'third agers' rather than more dependent 'fourth agers'.

- Corporate worship was also seen as very important, especially the music used and the space allowed for prayer and contemplation. Enjoying known hymns and seeking the presence of God were rated equally highly. 'Appropriate sermons' were also much appreciated. Various changes in worship style were cited as upsetting by some churchgoers and church leavers, especially in those groups meeting in the north of England.

- Two of the groups strongly felt that older people's needs were often overlooked in favour of those of younger people. Generally participants did recognise the importance of young people and valued a mixed-age church family or regretted the absence of young people. 'Older people have experience to contribute, younger people exuberance,' was the comment of one participant. However, they did not want to lose the expression of Christianity they were used to, especially within worship. A typical comment was: 'I think that the older people will come anyway; we've got to find ways of getting the younger ones to come, but still leave something we enjoy.'

- The various physical needs of older people in attending church (transport, ability to hear and see) were raised in all the groups and it was felt that churches do not address them adequately.

- Participants were glad when their absence from church was noted and followed up and were happy to use their gifts in church and community, especially in rural areas where there is a dearth of young people.

- There were very few overtly theological issues raised. Indeed a considerable number expressed the view that you don't need to go to church to be a Christian. However, most clearly saw the Christian message and way of life as being challenging rather than escapist.

- Changes in the church evoked almost equal responses for and against!

- The changes most desired by those attending included that there should be more shared worship between those of different denominations (though the churchgoers still valued their own denomination) and that churches should have a clear sense of direction and be more outward looking.

- When asked about the importance of 'vision' in the church, they viewed this in terms of present mission and service rather than in relation to the future.

Towards the end of 1999 Christian Research also carried out an extensive quantitative survey by means of a questionnaire (Appendix 5) in order to ascertain the extent to which older people feel marginalised or affirmed in local churches. Steps were taken so that respondents would be chosen randomly and an appropriately balanced mix be achieved denominationally, geographically, environmentally and according to size of congregation. Five denominations were selected which between them included 87% of English churchgoers over the age of 65: Church of England, Roman Catholic, Methodist, Baptist and United Reformed Church. A line between the Wash and the Severn distinguished churches in the north from those in the south. The environmental areas comprised City Centre (also including Inner City and Council Estates), Suburban, Town and Rural. A balance was sought between congregations under and over 100.

From the responses received it can be asserted that there was reasonable success in achieving the balances indicated above. The north-south division was 47%:53% (nationally 35%:65%). The environmental distribution –

of one third rural, just over one third suburban and just under one third other locations – reveal an increase of 10% (rural) and a reduction of 6% (town) when compared with the figures produced by the 1989 English Churches Census, which, however, related to churchgoers of all ages. Peter Brierley, Executive Director of Christian Research, comments: 'The difference in the rural percentages . . . reflects the many more elderly people going to church in rural areas, and fewer in towns and city centres.' The 57% Anglican respondents is much greater than the national percentage and the 4% Roman Catholic very much less; otherwise the denominations are accurately reflected. Church size at 60% under and 40% over 100 is within 5% of national figures.

In order to ensure a statistically acceptable response a very large number of ministers were approached for their help. Each was asked to distribute five envelopes to individual church-attenders aged 60 or over. Each of these in their turn was asked to pass on a similar envelope to another older person who, as far as they were aware, was a non-churchgoer. A grand total of 2,726 questionnaires were distributed achieving a highly commendable 77% response rate (2,093 forms).

The key variant built into the methodology is, of course, the distinction between churchgoers and non-churchgoers. Seven hundred and thirty non-churchgoers responded compared with 1,363 churchgoers. It transpired that 37% of the former in fact claimed to go to church at least monthly (compared to 97% of the churchgoers), a further 12% several times a year, and a quarter reported that they used to attend. This group was, therefore, not so clearly differentiated from the other as might have been desirable. However, in the responses to several key questions the distinction is apparent.

Three further 'control variables' were included in the questionnaire, relating to gender, age and marital status so that any significant variants in these areas could be identified. The responses revealed a gender division of 36% male and 64% female, which is within 1% of the outcome in the 1989 English Church Census and close to the national figures of 40% and 60% respectively. The average age of respondents, whether churchgoers or not, was approximately 72 though a response of only 10% was forthcoming from those over 85. More than half were married, a third widowed (10% less than in the population at large) and some 12% either single or divorced.

Detailed application of the findings of the qualitative survey and of the statistical data from the quantitative survey will be made as appropriate in the chapters that follow. Each chapter will also make suggestions seeking to help churches wishing to reduce the sense of exclusion felt by some older people and enhance their sense of belonging.

Providentially, during the course of our work we were able to benefit from three pieces of research done by others in areas overlapping with our concern. The first is contained in the report *Religion, Spirituality and Older People* by Kenneth Howse [6] who sifted the research findings in the USA since 1961 concerning the connection of religion, old age and well-being, identifying key questions and giving pointers for similar investigations in the UK, where such research material to date as assembled by Howse is rather more sparse. He gives considerable emphasis to the role and contribution of churches both in terms of pastoral care and in relation to public policy. In his Foreword Professor Peter Coleman expresses the hope that Howse's work will stimulate further investigation. We offer this book as a modest contribution from within the Christian faith community.

The second area of investigation of relevance is the work of the Church Leaving Applied Research Project initiated by Philip Richter and Leslie Francis, which sought to identify significant factors in church leaving and returning. The outcome was published as *Gone but not Forgotten.* [7] The initial random telephone survey appeared to indicate that, whereas 62% of the population of England claimed to have attended church at least six times a year at one time or another, three out of five of them no longer do so.

They see this as the biggest challenge facing the Church today, especially if (as they believe) those more likely to return than others can be identified.

Continuing their research, qualitative data was obtained from 27 in-depth interviews, of whom only three were with people over 50 years of age (one being over 70). The quantitative data derived from over 800 church leavers identified from a random selection of names in the London area phone book. The response rate was over 50% and of these 29% were aged 60 or over. Apart from the age spread there are other significant differences when compared with our own research. Their published data does not reveal whether the older respondents left church long ago (in which case their reasons would be historic not contemporary) or more recently. Their 198 suggested reasons for leaving are much more specific and comprehensive than our broader categories. More importantly, our research was largely concerned with older people who still consider that they belong to churches but feel left out and we were interested to discover the positive factors that help many of them to feel that they still do belong.

Nonetheless the published findings are very revealing and permission was sought to access the detailed data. Professor Francis informed us that work was continuing and that they had now received a total of 190 responses from people over 60 and a further 151 over 70. We were grateful for the secondary analysis of this consolidated data in relation to older people which was made available to us in June 2000. The data helpfully categorises respondents into three age groups (under 40, 40-59 and 60 plus) compared with the very broad division of those under and over 20 used in their book.

The third project is the 20-year study of 340 ageing people carried out by Professor Peter Coleman and completed in the autumn of 2000 which reveals the progressive decline in their allegiance to the Christian faith and the Christian Church. [8] This accords with the findings of Richter and Francis, which were consistent in all age groups, that half of all church leavers in their study confessed that the Church had lost its meaning for them.

Where relevant, cross-references are made to these research findings in the chapters that follow. References have otherwise been kept to a minimum because neither of our main source documents, the qualitative and quantitative reports produced for us by Christian Research, have been generally published. Further information can be obtained, if required, from Methodist Homes who hold the copyright for the reports.[9]

---

**References**

1 *Ageing*, Church House Publishing, 1990.

2 Albert Jewell (ed), *Spiritual Perspectives on Ageing*, Methodist Homes, 1998.

3 For full list of Halley Stewart booklets see select book list at Appendix 5.

4 Jackie Treetops, *Holy, Holy, Holy*, Faith in Elderly People (Leeds), 1996.

5 Albert Jewell (ed), *Spirituality and Ageing*, Jessica Kingsley, 1998.

6 Kenneth Howse, *Religion, Spirituality and Older People*, Centre for Policy on Ageing, 1999.

7 Richter and Francis, op. cit.

8 Peter G Coleman, *Stability and change in religious attitudes with ageing in a 20 year longitudinal study*, paper delivered to British Society of Gerontology Conference, September 2000.

9 Contact Senior Chaplain, Methodist Homes, Epworth House, Stuart Street, Derby DE1 2EQ.

# Chapter Two

# DRIFTING

*I used to go to mass every morning, and then into town to do a spot of shopping but ever since the doctor put me on these 'water pills' I dare not go to church, as it is at that time I need to visit the toilet so regularly. So now I just go into town. I miss going to mass but I'm sure God understands.*

Here is a woman who is by no means unique. She is drifting away from church, not through any conflict with the minister or changes to her own belief system, but due to a very simple problem – this church does not have a 'discreet' enough solution to 'what happens if a member of the congregation needs to go to the toilet during mass?'– in her case more than once during mass.

*There are so few people at daily mass, I would be too embarrassed to walk down to the front and open the door, which makes such a noise. They would all know where I was going – imagine having to do that more than once!*

There could be some quite simple solutions to this problem if only the church knew there was a problem in the first place. Does mass have to be at that time in the morning? Could the door be made less noisy? Could there be a more 'congregation-friendly' place to provide a toilet, at the back of church? Could the parishioner negotiate with her doctor a different regime for taking her pills?

Here is just one of the remarkably varied reasons why people may drift away from church attendance due to their personal circumstances which Richter and Francis discovered to be the case in at least a third of church leavers. They comment:

> For those who do attend, churchgoing usually becomes a habit – a good habit, but a habit

nonetheless. Like most habits, churchgoing can be disrupted by sudden changes in a person's life.[1]

If for many people going to church is indeed a good habit and churches want to help those people continue or renew the habit, it makes sense to first discover what the 'changes and chances' are that lead to people drifting away so that these may be addressed. The Richter and Francis study, of course, covered church leaving and returning throughout all age groups but this book wants to identify the particular reasons why older people leave. Most of this information has been provided by the quantitative research carried out for us by Christian Research and is summarised thus by Peter Brierley:

> It shows the key reason why people stop attending church is the death of their spouse. More than half, 54%, said this was why they stopped.
>
> Family responsibilities were the next most common cause, affecting 30% of respondents. Then came a generalised group of one in 5 or 6 of respondents, who said they left for no particular reason, or were disillusioned or moved.
>
> Finally there were 16 specific reasons which affected smaller numbers of respondents. One of these, 'death of someone close to me' (other than spouse or partner) was more important for town folk than others. It affected 14% of them against 2% of those living in rural areas, suburbs or city centres, and was one of only two factors in the whole survey in which church environment was a significant variation!
>
> Some reasons were not listed specifically but were written in as 'other reasons' . . .
>
>> impact of the war, working on Sundays, spouse disliking church attendance, leisure interests, living overseas, unfriendly people, boring services and known drifting. Further reasons included: 'not having nice clothes',

'laziness', 'Catholic v C of E tension', 'divorced so couldn't go', 'pursued other religions', 'church closed', 'afraid of the church' and 'I began to think rationally!' The reasons for stopping church did not vary by denomination.

This gives a very good overview of the reasons why older people leave church. We may all identify personally with some of them and be able to see where some of the solutions lie. Now, by examining in more depth some of the myriad personal circumstances which befall people during their later journey through life, we can hopefully identify some of the simpler steps to make church attendance easy and desirable. The bigger steps relating to patterns of fellowship and worship, in-depth pastoral care and the credibility of faith are explored in other chapters.

The 'changes and chances' which initiate a falling away from the church, and which lead to people losing touch with the church by default rather than intention, may best be grouped into three main categories of circumstance:

Physical factors – both of the church and the older person
Family – relationships and responsibilities
Illness – including dementia.

## PHYSICAL FACTORS

### Accessibility
The physical structure of the church may well be the first obstacle to continued regular attendance for increasingly frail people. I know, from my own recent experience, of family members who were unable to attend a funeral owing to the 'mountain' of steps to be negotiated at the front of the church. There was a side entrance with fewer steps but even that proved to be too difficult as it is at the bottom of a steep slope, which on this occasion was slippery due to a recent spell of snow! This same church had just undergone a huge refurbishment of the space directly underneath the mountainous steps. Much money

was spent on the modernisation to provide a parish centre to host social events, particularly youth-related events – what a shame that a lift wasn't included in the plans enabling people to enter the church from ground level.

Accessibility may present a problem even before arriving on church premises. The church needs to consider a strategy for transporting people with mobility problems from home to church. There are many reasons why older people may not be in a position to make their own way to church. They may be unable to walk the distance because of problems with their limbs or even their breathing. They may be unable to drive the distance as low income may preclude owning or using a car. It could be that a partner was the car driver and this mode of transport is lost if the partner dies. Maybe coming to church alone when the person has enjoyed a lifetime of coming with family is too much to bear. Does anyone in the church bother to find out?

Whatever the reason, transport to and from church, or even simply company to and from church, should not be too difficult a strategy to develop. A request from the pulpit or via the church newsletter should initiate some kind of congregational participation or rota. If your church is not fortunate enough to have sufficient car-drivers there may be a local 'Dial a Ride' or similar community transport scheme.

But does your church really know who needs a lift? Older people themselves are often too reticent or fiercely independent to ask for help. One frail elderly lady we spoke to told us that very occasionally she got a lift home from church but she didn't know what she would do when she could not make it up the hill any more: 'I can't afford to get a taxi every week on a pension, and it doesn't seem right. I will just have to stop going soon, the hill is too hard.' Nobody had noticed that she was struggling. Lack of mobility can become one of the first means of exclusion for the older person.

## Comfort

Once in church there may still be unwelcoming factors to be considered. How comfortable is it to spend time in the building? Is it too hot (or more likely too cold!)? Are the seats comfortable? Is the seating too close together, or too rigid? Is there anything to hold on to to help getting to the standing position? Some older people have joints and limbs that will not bend easily or 'fold' magically to let them squeeze into too small or restricted areas. If you are planning to refurbish, do consult older members of the congregation and let them try out the alternatives.

Of course, a welcoming church is more than just one that is physically accessible and reasonably comfortable:

*I had always been a good 'chapel girl' in my youth and continued with fairly regular church attendance until I married in my late 40s. My husband did not believe in God so I stopped going. We were only married a few years when he died, but as my mother took ill at about the same time all my attention was given to her. I continued to live like a good Christian and prayed alone. When my caring duties came to an end I looked forward to going back to church. I was in my 60s now and not as mobile as I used to be, my main handicap being arthritis in my knees, so I decided to try the nearest church – we all believe in the same God after all. The church was small with just a handful of people in it and I stayed near the back. I did not dare kneel down as I could not guarantee being able to get back up under my own steam. At the end of the service a member of the congregation who had been sat behind me came up to me, I presumed she was going to welcome me into the flock. She did say it was nice to see me, but also pointed out the parts of the service when I should have been kneeling. I haven't been back to that church. In fact it was a few years before I ventured into any church, but I have found a nice church since, just a little further down the road.*

There are a number of different issues in that story: physical disability, bereavement, family responsibilities, fellowship or the lack of it, all of which will be explored later in this and other chapters. But for now, what simple steps could have been taken to avoid that particular confrontation? Even ensuring that the seating is more comfortable may not solve all the problems since kneeling down may simply be out of the question for some knees! However, permission not to kneel (and equally permission not to stand) may be a simple solution. At a recent ecumenical service to celebrate Alzheimer's Awareness Week, it was obvious that there were visitors of all ages and denominations in the church hosting the event. It was also very probable that some of the congregation were non-churchgoers. At the outset of the service the welcoming minister simply invited people to sit, stand or kneel as they wished throughout the service. Similar suggestions can be made at other services.

At the church in the above less happy story with such a small congregation it would surely be easy to identify a new face, so it was a pity the 'welcome' was left to apparently the least welcoming of people! Some would argue that the most important job at church services is that of welcoming those who come; great sensitivity and awareness is required. What happens after the initial welcome is also of paramount importance and this will be covered in chapter three.

## Disability

A church which has always seemed adequate to parishioners may only start to look forbidding when the physical factors affecting the older person are also considered. Ageing can bring with it deterioration through slow and subtle changes. Many of these changes can be compensated for in church to alleviate some of the problems. Some older people have trouble hearing so the use of a good public address system will assist many, and the inclusion of an audio loop system will hopefully attend to the needs of the rest (provided they are encouraged to use the t-setting on their hearing aids). Some older people may have poor sight so, if large-print hymn and service books aren't available, maybe someone could produce that day's hymns and responses in large print on a computer and print out on card for distribution as required. There is little incentive for older people to go to church if they can neither hear nor see what is going on!

This chapter began with an illustration of how medication can determine one of the basic functions of the body, but even without an underlying heart condition the excretory functions of the body may be less 'predictable' as we age. It is worth repeating that the church needs to offer toilets which are easily located and accessible.

**Moving house**
The final physical circumstance I would like to examine is that of people who find themselves in a new home or environment. Our Christian Research survey revealed that about a fifth of respondents stopped going to church because they had moved house. This is not too dissimilar to the information derived from secondary analysis of the consolidated data collected by Richter and Francis where the equivalent proportion for those over 60 (many of whom could, of course, have moved much earlier) is almost a third. Moving house has the effect of breaking an existing pattern of life and church attendance may no longer be a 'given'. Richter and Francis comment that:

> Whenever churchgoers, of any age, move to a new community it may take them some time to re-establish links with a local church. To start with, they must hunt around to discover which churches are available locally, or within convenient travelling distance.[2]

Such hunting around becomes less practicable for those who are very old.

They go on to observe:

> Even when they locate a suitable church there are, however, other hurdles to negotiate. They will need to overcome any apprehension they may have as a 'newcomer' and summon up the courage to walk into a strange church . . .

> Assimilating into a new church is especially difficult for single or elderly people . . . maybe because they do not have the excuse of going to 'family things.' [3]

Research in the United States suggests that it takes five or more years to put down roots in a new church and there is no reason to think that this is very different in the United Kingdom. [4] Those who move may not be sufficiently motivated to make the transition and older people may not have five active years remaining in which to do so.

How can a church begin to cross this physical gulf and reach older (and other) people new to the area? Churches may, of course, arrange special services for older people at convenient times and with transport and refreshments duly laid on, but such 'segregation' has its obvious drawbacks. The best opportunities may be linked to the main festivals throughout the year, Easter, Christmas and Harvest in particular. These are times when newcomers of any age may feel that they stand out less. A leaflet drop in the area (which may best be done on an ecumenical basis) can advertise the date and time of the celebrations and services and assure people of a warm welcome (which must, of course, actually happen!). These would presumably need to go to all residents and not discriminate towards new arrivals. Older people who have got out of the habit of churchgoing perhaps long ago but wish to make a new start will be amongst those who respond. Once the invitation has been taken up the church may then be able to provide the new friends, fellowship and opportunities for worship that some will be seeking.

However, it is not always appreciated by churchgoers that the threshold into the worshipping congregation may appear impossibly high to those outside even if they have a will or yearning to come back. This is where a church-based lunch club for older people can act as a bridge, bringing them onto church premises and allowing them to meet church members. Such lunch clubs are often especially appreciated by older men. More about lunch clubs and about further opportunities for socialising and fellowship will be found in the next chapter.

It may also be the case, however, that moving house provides the impetus actually to 'free' the person from attendance at church. Richter and Francis comment: 'Where people have been over-involved in the church, a sense of "burn-out" may motivate their church leaving.'[5] Approaching half of all their respondents admitted that churchgoing had become a chore for them and that this was a factor in their ceasing to attend. In some cases, therefore, there may be a determined effort to 'get out of the habit' of going to church, and not being known in the new congregation allows the person to drift away without too great a sense of guilt or the reproach of other members of the congregation to which they belonged before moving. This need for space must be respected until such time as changing circumstances and recognition of need may again point them back to the Christian community. Whilst the church should offer the opportunity to attend and belong to new arrivals and welcome them, it is, of course, down to the individual to take up that invitation and respond.

**Going into care**
There is one type of move that the church may be mistaken in thinking does not require any effort on their part – that of a move from a private dwelling into a nursing or residential home. The church may consider that, once an individual has moved into a care facility, then all their needs are catered for, particularly in this present climate which emphasises residents' choice and rights. Attention to 'religious, cultural and spiritual needs' are included in most Community Care Charters.

In practice, however, there is a vast variation in how these needs are met. Many homes rely upon the input of visiting church ministers and church groups who can exercise a most valuable ministry in keeping older people in touch with their own spiritual roots and the wider community. Even in the best homes – those that do offer opportunities for worship, prayer and fellowship and sometimes chaplaincy – it should be recognised that an individual resident may want to retain links with their former church, either in preference to, or in addition to the services offered in the care home. Ensuring that this can happen should be the joint responsibility of the home and the church. The pastoral implications are pursued further in the next chapter.[6]

## Summary

This has not been an exhaustive description of the physical obstacles to attendance at church but has hopefully raised a greater awareness of some of the most common. The following is a most useful check-list for local churches formulated by Jeffrey Harris in Halley Stewart Booklet 10[7] who writes:

> A few years ago churches, along with other institutions, were reminded of the need to cater for disabled people: avoiding steps wherever possible, providing ramps, lifts and disabled toilet facilities etc. It was a much needed reform. Churches also need to check that they help frail and ageing members of the congregation in every way possible.
>
> Here are nine important questions to address, though it is not an exhaustive list:
>
> - Are the church buildings easy of access to those who are disabled or frail?
> - Do we have a transport system to bring older people to services and other church activities?
> - Are there available large print copies of prayer books and hymn books for those who are not now able to read normal size print?
> - Are the sound and loop systems in good working order so that those whose hearing is impaired can join fully in worship?
> - Are we sensitive to the needs of those who cannot kneel to receive Communion

or who find it difficult to stand for more than a minute or two?  There are liturgical reasons for standing at some points in worship but can we avoid causing frail members undue embarrassment or distress?

- Are toilets clearly indicated and located so that access is easy for those who may have need to use them frequently?
- When coffee etc is served after services and events so that people can circulate, are we aware of those who would wish to participate fully but find it difficult to stand or hold cups – so are chairs and small tables available for them at strategic points?
- Do we ensure that housebound people receive the church notices, newsletters and magazines?
- Is it possible to record services for the benefit of those who can no longer attend?

Positive answers by local churches to such questions will go a long way towards dealing with some of the most common changes and chances that tend to come with ageing so that older people who already belong and those who are newcomers may feel truly welcome.

## FAMILY RELATIONSHIPS AND RESPONSIBILITIES

### Bereavement
We have noted the clear finding of the quantitative research that by far the most common reason why older people stop attending church is the death of a spouse.  The research also revealed that many of those who had ceased attending church because of such bereavement did eventually return following their 'wilderness period' but they did not always have a good experience either of the funeral process or of receiving adequate continuing pastoral

care. This pastoral challenge is more fully addressed in the next chapter.

## Marriage breakdown

Another change in family relationships which can have a significant effect on established routines of churchgoing is marital breakdown and divorce. What the Church can do about welcoming divorced people back into church may well be seen as a doctrinal or faith issue rather than simply as responding to a change in personal circumstances. Churches need to be specially sensitive to those who find themselves in such a situation. Older people in particular may perceive being divorced as a reason for their exclusion from church, either because they themselves feel failures or because they expect the church to be condemnatory. 'Divorced so couldn't go' was the succinct comment of one of our respondents. Such alienation can last for many years and sometimes never be overcome. Even those divorced people who still feel welcome in church may experience split loyalties, because Sunday may be the main day when they are able to have contact with other family members.

## Family caring

Secondary analysis of the data gathered by Richter and Francis shows that over a third of all respondents attribute their leaving church at least in part to increased family commitments. Caring for family members can be time consuming and exhausting, especially when it is not in the 'natural' sequence of events. For example, when a young couple who are churchgoers marry and have children it is usual then to attend church as a family, though it is also not uncommon for this to be a time when churchgoing is disrupted or ceases, sometimes for a very long period. Over two thirds of all the respondents in the research of Richter and Francis reported that they simply got out of the habit of church attending.

However, if the children in question are your grandchildren and the only day you do not have some responsibility for them is Sunday you may feel you have other things you need to do with your time than get up and go to church.

*I used to enjoy going to church, I liked the music and the coffee afterwards and the chance to talk to old friends. I was never terribly regular in my attendance – not every Sunday, you understand, but it was a pleasure to go when I fancied it. But for the last two years I have been looking after my daughter's little girl. I have her from early morning until tea-time five days a week and sometimes on a Saturday night. By Sunday morning I feel I just need to unwind at home and prepare for the next week. I do sometimes miss church but my rest is more important at the moment.*

Here is a woman who is by no means unique. There must be an army of 'grans' and 'grandads' in the wider community enabling mothers to return to the workforce, and for many that work is full-time. Such responsibility can be demanding and exhausting.

*I often think when she goes to school and I have more time on my hands I will take up some of my former interests, but as I was never a regular churchgoer it seems 'cheeky' to go back after all this time.*

Of course, the church can hardly be held responsible for all family arrangements but it may be in a position to offer people links with the church other than attendance at service on a Sunday. If this woman was able to attend a playgroup or a mothers/grandmothers-and-toddlers' group organised in the church hall she might feel as if she is still nurturing links with the church and, therefore, not so 'cheeky' at resuming attendance on a Sunday when the time is right.

If caring for children is one of the reasons why people 'get out of the habit' of going to church, it may also be the case that it can bring people into church! This can be so for younger parents.

*I was brought up a Presbyterian, I went to Sunday school as a girl, but my parents were not regular churchgoers, but we prayed and often read the Bible at home. When I married I took instruction in the Catholic faith and promised to bring my children up Catholic. My husband was a 'lazy Catholic' so it was always me who took the girls to church. Once the youngest was old enough to go on her own I stopped attending. Now I'm housebound I am unable to attend church, but I do not mind, God is not only in church, my faith is strong and I can still pray privately and read my Bible if I want.*

In her case, though she retained her personal faith, her connection with the church effectively ended when her children were grown up. In other cases grandparents can find grandchildren a positive incentive for returning. Many older people, the great majority of whom themselves attended Sunday school or church in their early years, may wish to encourage their grandchildren to do the same and go with them.

Older people are not only called upon to care for fit and lively grandchildren. Thanks to the emphasis upon care in the community, people who are disabled or very frail mentally or physically are increasingly unlikely to go into care homes. Recent statistics reveal that 75% of long-term care is provided by families, mainly women, and 42% of such carers are themselves over retirement age. Sometimes caring for a relative may be as little as helping them with the heavier household tasks, or bringing in their weekly shopping. They may be able to live alone and function well enough in their own home but feel vulnerable outside, so need company or transport to get out. These days even the most disabled and vulnerable people are facilitated to remain in their own home, if they wish, which can mean 24-hour attendance on the part of a family member or members.

Very often it is a case of the old caring for the very old. Such family carers can easily become captive to the needs of the person being cared for. In these cases respite care can be offered by the Health or Social Services either in the form of a week or two's temporary stay in a care home for the one being cared for or in the provision of a few hours' relief. Sometimes this is good and flexible, but it can often be patchy and inadequate and may even be refused! When care is continually provided without adequate periods of respite the carer can become isolated and resentful as well as exhausted and they may have to give up or reduce their own pastimes and interests, including church attendance and activities.

What can churches do to help in these cases? A very great deal! Jeffrey Harris has covered this issue in full in Booklet 9 in the series of Halley Stewart Booklets, [8] but here is a summary:

> Churches are great sources of human contact as well as divine comfort. However, carers are frequently unable to get to church services and fellowship groups because of their caring commitment – unless others enable this to happen. This will, of course, mean some measure of self-sacrifice on the part of fellow Christians who will need to deny themselves in order to benefit the carer, but an informal rota of helpers can go a long way. Otherwise carers come sadly to feel that even the church does not care – at least not about them!

He goes on to list a few practical suggestions:

- Church premises can be made available for lunch clubs and other activities for older people. They need to get away from their carer from time to time just as the carer needs respite!
- Likewise, transport is appreciated so that older housebound persons can get to church activities on occasions whilst they are still able and out into the wider world. (This again can give invaluable respite to the family carer.)

- In the liturgies of the churches there is space given to remembering in prayer the needs of those who are sick in body or mind and the disabled, but the invisible army of carers needs to be prayed for too.

- Pastoral visitation can sometimes omit older persons with permanent carers, or concentrate on the one receiving care to the virtual exclusion of the carer. They need to be well and truly included, and if visitation and home communion can be provided by a small group, so much the better for all involved.

- Members of the church, as well as family and friends, need to recognise that caring for the carers is more than just thinking about them. It means calling on them, befriending and empathising with them and being willing to offer such help as may be appropriate. Ringing up in an evening, after the one cared for has retired for the night, and asking if it is convenient to call round for half an hour just to talk, gives a break from the feeling of loneliness and isolation experienced by carers. At the end of a difficult day it can relieve the stress and bring a degree of relaxation, even laughter. The giving of time to a carer is the precious gift without price-tag.

One of the conditions which results in an individual requiring full-time care is, of course, dementia. I will explore that condition in greater length in the next section.

## ILLNESS

Richter and Francis comment:

Ill health at any age can make it difficult for someone to get to church or to sit through a service and hence tends to disrupt their pattern of churchgoing. [9]

We have already covered the progressive deterioration in the senses and basic bodily functions which can cause inability to attend church or embarrassment while there or even reduce the enjoyment of a service. This section will simply seek to raise awareness of how suffering from either acute or chronic ill health may precipitate a drifting away from church.

*My hearing was failing and my wife had poor eyesight, we both were becoming less mobile but we still tried to manage church on a Sunday. After all, it had taken us a great deal of effort to find this particular church when we moved here, that offered the old style service and we had grown friendly with the vicar. But when I fell downstairs and later was admitted to hospital with a bleeding ulcer we could not make the enormous effort required to make it back to church. Luckily we were missed and someone from the church visited us and now we have a small service for family and friends in our house once a month – we know we are very lucky.*

This seems a great success story and an example to hold up to other churches. But what happened may not be to everyone's liking, and the experience of many older people will in any case be different. I myself do not attend my own church every Sunday. I am pleased the congregation is large, in fact that I am not missed. Having someone call on me to see where I was on any given Sunday would fill me with dread as if I were being checked up on! But I may be somewhat over-sensitive. There is surely some merit in being missed from church and people caring enough about you to call and ensure you receive what you want from the church.

A survey in the USA concluded that those who drop out of church wait on average six to eight weeks and if they are not missed their time will be re-engaged on other activities.[10] Older frail people, of course, do not have this option and may already be feeling very marginalised. Hopefully churches will have a policy to cover visiting the sick and housebound. What needs to be developed is a sensitive way to know when people are not attending church because they are sick, especially for people who live alone and do not have family to inform the church. For those remaining within the church's fellowship a system of regular ringing round from one person to another may work well and should pick up instances of ill health. Since such people may have ceased to attend church because of their ill health years ago, reaching them may require a leaflet drop of literature stating that the church cares and including a phone number or a postal return slip to be returned if the recipient would like a home visit.

Conversely, illness may actually initiate a return to church. At such times when we become increasingly aware of our mortality we tend to think more about the purpose and destiny of our lives. Some people who have got out of the habit may start to re-engage with their faith practice when they are admitted to hospital. Even if they are an in-patient for a short space of time, they may have availed themselves of the services of the hospital chaplain and/or attended the hospital chapel. They may wish to continue this new or renewed faith practice when they are discharged, and it is to be hoped that hospital chaplains can provide a referral encouraging an introduction or re-introduction to their local church. How well such people returning to church are received will, of course, determine whether or not they stay.

The church will have to examine how sensitively they welcome people suffering any form of illness into their church. As a child I remember a priest who would draw attention to you if you coughed during the service, and on occasion would ask you to leave. But that would not happen now – would it?

**Dementia**
There is one particularly isolating condition that needs some exploration here to make sure that churches are doing their utmost to make people with it, and their carers, feel welcome. This is dementia, which can be one of life's most terrible 'changes and chances'. Dementia is an organic disease and not the natural consequence of ageing. The term dementia refers to a collection of symptoms which reveal themselves in deteriorating brain function. It

is the result of various disease processes affecting the brain, the most common of which is Alzheimer's disease.

However, the actual cause of dementia is not usually what concerns most people, they are more concerned with the symptoms of the disease. The most common of these are: loss of memory, particularly for recent events, dis-orientation in time and place, difficulties with verbal communication, and changes in behaviour and sometimes in personality. The outcome is almost inevitably increasing isolation. Most dementia illnesses are progressive and irreversible. This means that the person with the condition and their carer will need more support, contact and compassion as the disease progresses, not less! Although the person with dementia may appear to have changed irretrievably they still have a great capacity for feeling, and what was important or crucial to them may still remain so – even if they cannot transmit that to us.

Sadly, ministers and many church members may feel inadequate in relating to someone with dementia and this just increases their sense of isolation:

> *My husband had been deeply involved with the church all his life, and when it became too difficult to take him to church I enlisted the help of the local minister to visit us at home. He sat the entire time with his back to my husband apparently embarrassed. He whispered that one of his relatives had gone the same way and how sorry he was for me. He left without even saying a prayer as if it would have been useless – at the time it would have been the one thing that would have made perfect sense to my husband.*

Many people are still unaware of what dementia does to people, and the clergy cannot be expected to know *everything* about *everything*. However, as the numbers of very old people in this country continues to rise this is a condition that will become increasingly prevalent. The chance of developing dementia increases with age, from 5% of the population at the age of 65 to 20% amongst the over-80s. Since the age profiles of so many churches are high, this is a challenge that is not going to go away.

There is a great deal of stigma still attached both to having dementia and to looking after someone who has it. This stigmatisation may keep people out of church, often when attending church could offer so much to both the person and their carer. Congregations that can be amazingly understanding and tolerant of the noise and disruption sometimes caused by the presence of young babies and children are often quite the reverse when it comes to the 'challenging behaviour' of an older person with dementia. This can lead to the effective exclusion of both the older person and their family carer or carers.

Communication may be difficult but religious ritual can provide marvellous memory cues for people with dementia and participation in a well remembered ritual can promote feelings of comfort and the reassurance of God's unconditional love, and so increase well-being. The church must rise to this challenge of learning about the condition and finding ways of effective communication which will go a long way to avoiding the isolation felt by everyone touched by this condition. There are now lots of practical resources available to help people learn about the disease and its progress with tips on how to meet the needs of this group, not least their spiritual needs.[11]

**Summary**
The rest of this book will explore some of the deeper issues that lie behind why older people have stopped attending church. When the churches explore changes and challenges in areas such as spirituality and belief systems, fellowship and pastoral support, and not least styles of worship, and have agreed on appropriate strategies to encourage people back to church or to continue attending, I hope they will have given attention to some of the circumstantial and often more easily removed obstacles in the path of church attendance that have been raised here. What it requires to begin to stop the drift is the willingness to put oneself in the other person's shoes, to listen to what they say and to act appropriately.

**References**

1  Richter and Francis op. cit. p.65.

2  Ibid p.68.

3  Ibid p.69.

4  Wuthnow and Christiano, *The effects of residential migration on church attendance in the United States*, 1979, quoted in Richter and Francis op. cit. p.69.

5  Richter and Francis op. cit. p.92.

6  See also Alison Johnson, *Residential Care*, Christian Council on Ageing, 2000.

7  Listed in Appendix 6.

8  Ibid.

9  Richter and Francis op. cit. p.72.

10  Ibid p.25.

11  E.g. Halley Stewart Booklet No 7 listed in Appendix 6.

# Chapter Three

# BELONGING

## Introduction

What is it that gives older people a sense of worth and well-being in life? It perhaps needs underlining that their needs are basically the same as the needs of those who are younger. Whatever our age, we all need friendship and fellowship, to give love and to receive it, to feel valued and to know that if we were not there we would be missed. In other words, we need to feel that we do matter.

It is, of course, misleading to categorise all older people as 'over 65s' or 'pensioners'. They are far from being a homogeneous group. Dr Peter Brierley, in his research for our project, has used the following sub-categories: 'Third Agers', ie 65-74 year olds, who are usually active and do most of the volunteering within the community as well as in the church; those 75 to 84 who are the 'active frail'; and the 'less active elderly', aged 85 and over. Each of these different groups of older people needs to be considered as part of the whole Christian fellowship, but even so there remains an artificiality about any such groupings since individuals of all age groups vary so much one from another. Such an understanding should always lie at the heart of Christian pastoral care. Every individual, whatever their age, remains unique person.

There is, however, one thing that many older people have in common and that is an historic connection with the Christian Church. National figures show that between 54% and 36% of all children went to Sunday school between 1910 and 1940.[1] Those children have now reached the age when they are the older people in our society today. Sadly, however, they are not to be found in such numbers in our churches nowadays. Whereas 2.2 million older people watch *Songs of Praise*, only one in five older people claim to attend church once a fortnight. The reality may well be less, except in the case of black Pentecostal Churches where four in five older people attend worship on a weekly basis. Amongst Hindu and Muslim elders the numbers are even higher.

These figures suggest that the need for fellowship and belonging on the part of the majority of older people is not being met by churches and so many have ceased to belong. Although Kenneth Howse assembles evidence that people who hold religious belief and have religious involvement gain emotional and spiritual benefits that enhance their health and well-being ('church is good for you!'),[2] our own research indicated that the older a person was the less strong their sense of belonging when compared with their situation in time past.

Probably the major cause of the marginalisation of older people in churches is that they have lost that sense of 'belonging' – belonging to a family which in some ways substitutes for the natural family, and in other ways transcends it. Certainly this view was the most important one to emerge from the focus groups and surveys held in connection with our research. It confirms the findings of Richter and Francis' secondary analysis, the accumulated data of which reveals that in the case of nearly half of all church leavers they did not feel part of the church, the highest percentage being amongst those over 60.

Richter and Francis[3] point out:

> In a society of high geographical mobility and rapid change, the church can be a much-needed source of close friendships and supportive networks, especially for the isolated nuclear family and those living on their own. The church can even, as it were, take the place of a person's far-away family, offering support in times of crisis and a regular 'family' atmosphere. Human beings have an abiding need to feel that they belong somewhere. When churches fail to offer them this sense of belonging, people often prefer to leave.

They will find their need to belong met through some other group or activity where they will make new friends who may well not go to church. Sadly, in the case of older people their 'leaving' is more likely to be a case of being left out rather than making the choice to cease to belong. For the very old few alternatives to bring them a sense of belonging may remain.

This sense of belonging will tend to be fostered for people in three main ways:

- Through fellowship, giving the opportunity to meet with others socially and in Christian sharing.
- Through feeling affirmed in their intrinsic value, and in the gifts they still have to offer.
- Through the provision of sensitive pastoral care.

Under the above headings this chapter looks in particular at good (and less good) practice with a view to encouraging the local church to become in its own environment a spiritual oasis, a place (or community) offering spiritual refreshment and support for those on the journey into old age.

## BELONGING – THROUGH FELLOWSHIP

Fellowship brings the opportunity to meet with others socially and in Christian sharing. It is not always appreciated that such a sense of belonging may relate partly to the physical size of the building where the congregation worships. Over-large churches may seem impersonal and small ones claustrophobic. Individuals will be prone to leave if the particular balance between intimacy and anonymity to which they have become accustomed is disturbed, or if they move to a situation where the balance is different.[4]

This need for anonymity or intimacy is one that relates to people of all ages. It applies to a young woman who slips in at the back on a Sunday to attend the evening service, but disappears as soon as it is finished. The church never knew her name or her story, but she came frequently. It also applies to an older person drawn back into the church by the warmth and nostalgia experienced at a carol concert. After Christmas the man came tentatively to church one Sunday morning, to find not a church full of people, alight with Christmas spirit, but one half empty though with enough in the worship and welcome to be satisfying. At the end of the service he stayed for a cup of tea and chatted. He made himself known. In time he became more involved, re-establishing the church-going pattern of his youth.

People can also be put off from churchgoing because of what they perceive as the 'cliquey' nature of the church's fellowship, which may largely be a reflection of whether or not they feel that they belong. This was mentioned by a small number of respondents to the questionnaire that preceded the focus groups in our research and was recognised as a major issue at one of the groups. Secondary analysis of the data from Richter and Francis is more revealing in that 23% of all respondents, of whom over a quarter belonged to the over-60s, were disillusioned by local factions within the churches.

One of the churches that participated in our initial survey was a small one on the outskirts of Leeds. The fellowship there was remarkable as was the warmth of its welcome. It is used here, not as an ideal or perfect church, but as an example of good practice. Your own church may be very different, or perhaps quite similar, but hopefully some of the pointers that are drawn from this example will give you a check-list for your church and food for thought.

> This little church has 90 members, and meets in an old but refurbished chapel building, in a mainly residential area. The building is small, only just fitting the congregation that has grown from 40 to 90 in just five years. The chairs are comfortable and it has a sound system. The atmosphere is warm, physically as well as emotionally. Nobody comes and goes unnoticed. The congregation is a real family, a mixture of old and young, babies,

grandmothers, couples, singles, teenagers and children, who sit side by side, comfortably packed together. The worship is modern and old, loud and quiet, active and still, challenging yet sensitive. Young and old help to lead the worship and prayers. After the service there is a time for sharing over a cup of coffee. Most importantly not one older person feels at all marginalised, or uncared for.

There are many intergenerational activities where young and old share memories and opinions. One older person is responsible for sending a card to everyone on their birthday, another for sending a card or a letter to anyone who is sick. Yet other older people are part of a visiting team. One older person who is physically unable to attend the church any more is still able to phone to make contact with anyone in need and give support. People visiting her go away blessed and refreshed. The older people are involved in mid-week Bible study, house groups, fellowship groups. They have the wisdom and experience of life to contribute and a need to share, and this is welcomed.

The minister and the congregation show that they value the older people and are there to listen and to give a hand if required. Some of the congregation did an awareness course on the needs of those with dementia and set up a visiting team at a newly built home for people with dementia. The visitors, many of whom are themselves in their seventies, provide friendship and occasionally worship for the residents. The church also lives on a worldwide map.

This small growing church seems to have the balance right for good fellowship for both young and old. If we look at it more closely we may find insight into ways to enhance our church's own fellowship and sense of belonging, especially for the old.

- **Newcomers**
  The church we have highlighted is on the look-out for the total newcomer and for the old regular who might be missing, and has developed an effective policy to deal with both situations. The newcomer is sure of a sincere greeting as they come in, a friendly face to sit next to, and a warm welcome over coffee.

- **Age span**
  The church is fortunate in having a wide span of ages and is for many their extended family. This also means that there are enough fit and active older (and younger) people to support the very old and the housebound. A broad age span helps to give balance to a fellowship. Richter and Francis refer to an older church leaver who felt lost in a congregation made up mainly of young people and students: 'I just couldn't handle all these young happy people.'[5] They also show that the opposite can be true, the younger person feeling overwhelmed by so many older people: 'There are old people there (and) they (the young people) don't like old people.'[6]

- **Intergenerational activities**
  The church featured above has meaningful activities involving young and old people together in the church. The focus groups in our research revealed how much older people liked the intergenerational spread of the local church, especially contact with young people and children. Apart from worship and general social gatherings, shared practical activities can be fun and taped interviews with housebound people enlightening. Shared reminiscence between generations can be fascinating; a good starting-point for this is the sharing of 'Memory Boxes' into which individuals are encouraged to put those items that mean most to them personally and have lasting significance.[7] Such activities can contribute helpfully to 'all-age worship' or fit elsewhere into the church's activities programme.

- **Fellowship groups**
  The congregational members enjoy Bible study, house groups and the women's fellowship.  Research has shown that religious institutions are important in fostering durable and supportive interpersonal relationships.[8]  Many older people welcome the opportunity to belong to house groups and to provide hospitality for them.  In such groups they can get to know people of different ages, make friendships and share their Christian experience.  Care needs to be taken of course, to provide transport if required and to ensure that older people can both hear and contribute on equal terms with others.  Meetings in homes, with the associated socialising over light refreshments, can present a 'lower threshold' and a more relaxed atmosphere than entering a church building for more diffident people.

  Regular church-based meetings can provide same-age fellowship for older people too.  They can feel very at home in a group that is predominantly an older one, such as a women's fellowship, where they find a great deal of mutual support in bearing the various crises and challenges of later life.  Such a group can effectively become their 'church' even if they never get to Sunday worship.  Older men can present a greater challenge now that the days of church billiard and snooker rooms have largely passed and better facilities are available in pubs and clubs.  However, some churches discover an invaluable resource in their retired men-folk who can utilise their practical skills and find enjoyment working together as a team.

- **The wider community**
  The congregation is aware of the needs of those in the community, often working ecumenically, as in the project concerned with visiting people with dementia.[9]  Such a project fosters a sense of purposeful partnership and fellowship in those involved.  Another congregation, consisting almost entirely of older people, holds coffee mornings every Saturday and is able to give away many hundreds of pounds annually to community groups and good causes.  The horizons of older people

can easily shrink unless appropriate stimulation is provided.

- **The world Church**
  They live on a large map, keeping aware of the needs of the worldwide Church, offering financial, emotional and spiritual support to mission partners in the third world, as well as receiving information and feedback on the needs of children and old people in circumstances very different from their own. It is all too easy for church fellowship to become narrow, parochial and inward-looking.

- **Evangelism**
  In the broadest sense the surveyed church has real awareness and sensitivity to make the most of any opportunity to befriend, offer hospitality or evangelise – sometimes in quite surprising ways. Some years ago, when there was an excess of butter in the European community, the Government, in its wisdom, decided to give it away to older people. Up and down the country various halls were used for the distribution, and the members of this little church offered their premises. They wanted to make people feel welcome and decided to give everyone queuing a cup of tea and a biscuit. They set out tables with pretty tablecloths and flowers in the hall and served the refreshments whilst people were waiting. It was very much appreciated. The butter collection became a special social occasion and people stayed on chatting together. Ten older ladies joined the church following that event. They were all widowed, all had felt very lonely, and all had gone to church in the past but had been lost along the way. After many years these ladies are still affectionately known as 'the butter ladies'. Many older people are good at offering and receiving 'friendship evangelism', which research has consistently proved to be the most effective kind of evangelism because it flows so naturally.

If the experience of one small church in helping older people feel that they truly belong has been so positive, there is no reason why other churches should not do the same. The following questions should enable you to carry out a brief audit of the fellowship life of your church and will help to identify areas for action.

In your congregation/church:

- What arrangements are there for welcoming newcomers of whatever age?
- How wide and balanced is the age span? What strengths and weaknesses does this reveal?
- What opportunities are there for intergenerational activities, through which Andrew Cunnington suggests 'we can learn from one another, be blessed by one another and feel we are beginning to be one community rather than a lot of little ones'?[10]
- What fellowship groups are there which include older people?
- How do you cater for older men?
- What links are there that bring the church closer to older people in the community?
- Are there occasions which bring older people in the community onto your premises and, if so, is there real meeting with them?
- Do you support a missionary or third world project, and how do older people contribute to it?

**Mid-week activities**
The church we have featured is fortunate in that it provides ample opportunity for fellowship for older and younger people outside their Sunday worship programme. This subject deserves more attention here since mid-week meetings and events are a real growth industry in some churches.

One church has taken the initiative to employ a minister for the over 50s which they recognise as being their predominant age group. The worker in question is involved not just in setting up meetings that older people might enjoy, but rather seeks to focus on the deep need of every human being for belonging. The minister has developed a number of special interest groups which have grown out of people's particular gifts or hobbies. These groups include music, banner making, découpage, wildlife and pot gardening, to name but a few. They are not just for older people and are attended by people of all ages. These groups are promoting fellowship, a sense of belonging, and opportunities to utilise knowledge and gifts and to learn from one another. They also provide a very good support system for their members. Although run by the church, the groups are not exclusive but are open to non-churchgoers too. Welcomed and valued, those who haven't attended for many years can find a way back to church through such groups.

Mid-week day-time services have much to commend them to older people, provided they can get there. A warm corner can be created, with cushions on the seats. Those who attend can participate if they wish through helping to lead the prayers or doing the reading. A cup of tea or coffee can be available before or afterwards. One large cold church, with a Sunday congregation of about 150, has created such a cosy corner. Its mid-week service is brimming over with 25 people attending most weeks, predominantly belonging to the 60 plus age group. The service focuses a real sense of belonging, is short, quiet and reflective, and includes the sharing and celebration of personal anniversaries.

There are many variations on this theme, for example, a hymn sing-along of all the old favourites. A pianist to help is an asset, but if one is not available there are some very good taped hymns, and even computerised organs and keyboards that play themselves![11] Similar fellowship can be provided in local residential and nursing homes and is usually very much appreciated.

Many older people suffer from loneliness and may meet or communicate with very few other people from day to day. Luncheon clubs can be a great blessing for them providing a warm meal, conversation, friendship, and maybe a little entertainment or an occasional coach outing. However, whatever the church provides there will be those who say the church does not care. A man in his 80s at a city centre luncheon club was asked if he went to church. His gruff reply was, 'The church? No! The church has done now't for me!' Yet he was at a church luncheon club, had been brought by church transport, and was supported at home by volunteers from a Methodist Homes Live at Home Scheme! [12] Fellowship and support were being provided quietly and effectively. This is surely Christian caring at its best.

Does your church have regular fellowship meals, either on a Sunday or at some other time, say once a month or once a quarter? Lunch, tea or even breakfast shared with others is an ideal opportunity for breaking down the barriers of age or isolation. Such hospitality encourages fellowship and can be a great boon for those living alone.

## BELONGING – THROUGH AFFIRMATION

Wider society tends to be ageist in attitude and, in the graphic phrase of a 1980 Age Concern report, to shunt many older people from the main line into the sidings. [13] Churches are surely called to challenge such values and to manifest a very different attitude in their own congregational lives. [14]

When people remain involved in the life of the family, church or wider community, they retain a greater sense of belonging and purpose. Our research was encouraging in revealing that a high proportion of older people still in churches felt valued because they were wanted, loved and involved. As a consequence many of their gifts and talents were being used.

This is thoroughly in keeping with St Paul's picture of the Church as the body of Christ (I Cor 12:12-27) in which the contribution of each member is vital. However, ageist attitudes in society at large undermine older people's sense of value and purpose as they are seen to be manifestly second-class citizens, redundant in many regards. Sadly such attitudes can easily invade churches. On the other hand churches can appear ageist the other way, ie. as strongholds of older people with fixed ideas who do not affirm the contribution of younger people! Our investigations did reveal some tension regarding the affirmation that might be expected by the old over against the young. Some older people displayed enormous grace and had turned themselves inside out in order to accommodate the needs and desires of younger people. They deserve much credit. Others displayed real anger as revealed in the terse comment: 'We pay for the church!'

Some churches, of course, are made up entirely of older people and to keep the church alive they have to do all the tasks and take on all the roles. This is often the case in country districts. In other churches older people may find themselves devalued and de-roled. For them old age has been transformed into a role-less state. This can cause a profound loss of the older person's dignity and sense of belonging. One lady had helped to make the tea after worship for years. When, due to ill health, she could no longer do so, she sat at the side and watched others doing it. She felt lost, lonely and not wanted. Being waited on went against the grain! She needed to be doing. She had been part of the life and soul of the tea-making team and now very few people spoke to her.

That woman's feeling of marginalisation was the direct outcome of her personal frailty but it can become institutionalised. A London vicar in suburbia quotes how a swathe of very established middle-aged people left the church because their role had been taken by younger members. They felt redundant. [15] There is a close and fragile link between role and belonging, and great sensitivity is called for. Whilst some older people hang on to leadership positions in the church out of an unwillingness to let go, many do so for fear that there will be no one to take their place and would genuinely like to retire or have a change. To know when to retire is a real gift.

There is a need for churches to be specially sensitive to people as they come to 'retirement' from their main occupation in life, be that child rearing, homemaking, or work outside the home, because such a transition can be very threatening. Finding a new role, new interests and new friends can take a number of years. The retired person is in many ways free to choose, but choices do tend to decrease with age. So, whether it be someone retiring from their life's work or someone letting go of a role in church through age or ill health, a listening ear and support are required. They need affirming for what they have done, for what they can continue to do but most of all for who they are.

It is worth underlining that very many of our churches would fall apart without the wealth of talents and generous dedication of time that older people contribute. They have much to offer, whether they be active and bustling and still running a lunch club at 86 years old, or housebound and disabled. One such disabled and frail lady is remembered by her visitor with great affection. She could no longer attend church so tapes of the service and Bible readings were brought to her. She was very immobile but she loved to talk. Her visitor used to call to cheer her up, but in the end they both shared their problems, and both were uplifted and cheered. There was a healthy mutuality and reciprocation of need between a more active and a less active member of the body of Christ. It is this feeling of empowerment, self-worth, mutuality and belonging on the part of older people that churches should seek to encourage both in society and in the church. This is what is meant by 'affirmation'.

It is all the more affirming and enabling if older people can be encouraged to go on doing things for themselves. A group of residents in their late 80s and 90s at a Methodist Homes care home felt useless when there was little they believed they could do any longer. In consultation with the home manager they decided to meet for 20 minutes of silent prayer every morning around a lighted candle when they would remember those asking for or needing prayer. This became known in the wider community and now they receive requests from near and far and feel affirmed in having a continuing purpose. However, it should not be presumed that all older people necessarily have a special gift for prayer or desire to pray or that this is the only contribution they have to make!

Affirmation can legitimately become 'celebration' of the gifts of older people (alongside those of others) in the worship and life of the church: their wisdom, faithfulness, hobbies, life work, place in the family and natural gift for 'friendship evangelism'. It is sad that this continuing affirmation of their value and contribution is not, on the whole, as conspicuous in white British churches as it is in other ethnic and religious traditions.

There is, of course, one other very hidden and precious gift that very old people can bring to us, which is simply the gift of themselves, however frail or immobile or confused they may be. They bring themselves. In the end they can do no other. The very old and frail can teach us so much: about being rather than doing, about life and death, about our humanity, about perseverance, acceptance and letting go, about compassion, fear and hope. One West Indian lady in her 80s, who had had a number of major strokes and had been in hospital for six months, testified that she 'ran the race to get God's promise, the crown of eternal life'. Such commitment and radiant faith needs continual affirmation whilst the person is alive and not just in the funeral address!

The following is a list of just some of the activities and emphases which help to affirm older people as having significance and value. How many of them are reflected in the life of your church?

- Self-help groups
- Special interest groups
- Reminiscing groups
- Intergenerational activities
- Making a memory box and sharing it (see above)
- Writing and sending of birthday cards, get well cards, baptism cards

- Helping to devise special events and retirement services
- Keeping the congregation informed of the changing political scenario for older people and their needs
- Visiting one another and those in need
- Hospitality
- Practical tasks around the church
- Leading and attending fellowship groups and services
- Praying
- Life experience
- Being themselves
- Being present
- Being a forerunner and example for younger folk to follow
- Presenting a challenge and a reminder
- Acting as history makers and writers.

## BELONGING – THROUGH PASTORAL CARE

In the many conversations in which we engaged in preparing to write this book we discovered considerable anecdotal evidence to substantiate the statistical findings of Richter and Francis: that, of those leaving church later in life, one in four found the church uncaring, one in five felt let down when they needed support and one in six felt that ministers did not provide sufficient care.

Evidently the days are gone when most ministers or pastors visited everybody in their churches on a regular basis. [16] The main reason for this is sheer pressure, both of time and numbers. Priorities have to be clearly set. People today are living longer then ever before. The number of older people in our communities is increasing whereas the number of stipendiary ministers is decreasing. Time is at a premium. Even regularly taking communion to those no longer able to come to church may be beyond what a priest or minister can achieve if there is no lay assistance.

The Church has been waking up to the implications over the last two decades. Pastoral care can no longer just be the prerogative of the parish priest or local minister; it must be seen as the work of all the people in the church.

A familiar story is of the older person who says, 'Nobody from the church has been to see me.' Then it becomes known that somebody from the church called yesterday with some home-made buns and stayed to chat. Another person from the church has called with some flowers and stayed for a cup of tea today. 'Nobody from the church has been' means that the vicar or minister hasn't called. Only patient understanding and teaching will surmount this difficulty, as well, of course, as the pastor or minister knowing who is unwell or in crisis and visiting as appropriate.

**A strategy to cope**
Pastoral care will vary from place to place and according to the priorities of the church and the minister, the number of available volunteers and the time and energy they have. Some denominations have a strong tradition of lay visitation; for example, it is estimated that members of the Catholic Society of St Vincent de Paul carried out one million home visits in 1997.[17] However, not everyone will be suitable to offer pastoral support to older people, and training is necessary if it is to be done well. Pastoral care is most effective and efficient when the church knows the needs of its congregation and community, together with its own strengths and weakness, and establishes its own caring priorities and strategy.

There is, of course, a limit to the amount of pastoral care members of a congregation can be asked to offer.[18] It is important to recognise that, just as every minister cannot meet every need within the congregation, neither can every church meet every community need. To enhance such wider pastoral care it will be important to work in partnership with other agencies and other churches wherever possible. To effect this requires good leadership and an openness on the part of ministers.[19]

53

One local council of churches became aware of the needs of people with dementia. There was nothing in their locality for such people. So, after training was given to deepen their understanding of dementia, they set up a Friendship Club for people with dementia and their carers. The person with dementia and their carer are collected and brought to a prepared church hall. Other volunteers are there to talk and engage with the carer and the person with dementia. They may play games, or listen to music, or have a sing-along or just chat. This club is a new initiative which is working out very well, and it is a way of bringing fellowship to those in need and support to the carers. It came about because local churches were happy to work together, with support from 'the professionals', for the good of their community.[20]

### Care in life crises

As we have seen in the previous chapter there are many reasons why people leave churches. Our survey pinpointed some of the main reasons why people have left for at least a year. We reiterate them briefly here in order that ministers and churches can focus their limited pastoral resources upon some of the crucial life experiences of older people when they are at their most vulnerable.

### Moving house

This was a reason for having left the church given by a fifth of our respondents. Moving house or leaving home can be a dropping off point at various stages in life but lots of people choose to move around the time of their retirement from work. The transition is often far from easy. The church must make time to pass people's names on and help to make connections. Does yours? Likewise, receiving churches need to play their part with sensitivity, especially if the newcomer needs space for a while.

This is particularly important for the older person going into a nursing or residential home when it is sometimes believed that all their needs will be attended to. In fact for many it is a frightening, disorientating and extremely lonely experience. One man in a nursing home said, 'I used to be church warden and treasurer; now I am just thrown on the rubbish heap. Nobody visits me!' He was very angry. Sometimes such people simply fall off the church roll after a period of time and become totally lost to the church. Does yours keep an up-to-date list of all those in care homes and ensure that they receive adequate pastoral care?

**Illness**
This was mentioned as a reason for leaving by only 7% of our respondents. However, increased life expectancy necessarily means that older people face the prospect of longer periods of ill health. Most churches are alert to emergency situations and quick to visit and take flowers to people encountering acute illness, especially if they are admitted to hospital; far less so to chronic and progressive conditions such as arthritis, emphysema or increasing deafness and blindness. Moreover the current emphasis upon primary care means that fewer people are admitted to hospital and, when they are, it is usually for short periods. The needs of older people, therefore, can tend to be less obvious and so be overlooked by churches.

In the case of people with Alzheimer's disease and other forms of dementia, church people may be tempted to look the other way because they simply have no idea how to communicate. They may also be embarrassed and frightened. In fact what is most needed is simply continuing contact, friendship and support. One regular church attender developed Alzheimer's disease and was forgotten by the church. His wife said that in the early stages of the illness her husband would have welcomed a visit from his church friends but sadly no one came. She felt desperately disappointed and let down. 'The church doesn't care, does it?' was her indictment. Her question remains to be answered by every congregation.[21]

**Bereavement**
Those going through life crises such as hospitalisation, facing terminal illness or bereavement are especially vulnerable. In particular we have noted that 54% of those of our respondents who had at some stage left the church gave the death of their spouse as the main reason. The focus groups showed how important it was for pastoral

carers, especially the ordained minister, to show real sensitivity at such times of crisis. Insensitivity can lead to a breach that takes many years to heal, if at all.[22]

However, it is not always appreciated that older people tend to suffer a succession of bereavements other than the loss of a spouse or partner. The death of a member of the younger generation in the family can cause special grief linked with the sense that it would have been more appropriate if they themselves had died. The death of life-long or longstanding friends brings the added recognition that these are irreplaceable. Such losses of persons to whom they were close (other than partners) was reported by 14% of our respondents as a reason for ceasing to go to church. Curiously this affected many more people living in towns than in other areas and one can only speculate that such environments may be more 'anonymous' and less supportive for those who live there.

One woman of 60, Gladys, had a stroke and lost much of her mobility; within two months her husband, also 60, had died. Social Services arranged for her to go into a nursing home. Four months later her sister, who was her only living relative, died. In six months she had had four major bereavements: she had lost her health, her husband, her home and her sister. She was very angry and disturbed. She was a Christian and the home asked her if she would like to speak to a priest. She said yes. The priest came, and all Gladys could do was to shout angrily, 'Why did God do this?' The priest said, after just five minutes in her room, 'I am going now. When you have stopped shouting you can ask for me again.' Of course, she did not do so. It was months later when a deaconess visiting someone else passed by her room and said, 'Hello.' That deaconess then took the full force of the anger and the grief week after week. In time a befriender was found, a volunteer to take her on the occasional outing. Gladys is now a regular attender at the local church. Transport and a companion are always provided, and she has become a real favourite with many people. The outcome was so nearly very different from that.

Two men, Charles and Ben, one from a large city and one from a small town, both left the church after the death of their wife. Charles was 80 years old and had a lot of support from his family and the church. However, within months of his bereavement he stopped going to church even though folk were happy to take him. His daughter, who was a church member, offered to sit with him. No, in his grief he could not face it. As the months went by he became very ill and depressed, hardly going out at all. An elderly man of a similar age to Charles, a friend from church who had lost his own wife called, even though Charles didn't want visitors. The visits from this elderly friend, and the care and commitment of Charles' daughter, together with a good GP, have helped to ease Charles' burden. So, though he never returned to the church he never felt completely marginalised. His faith has remained and he finds comfort in watching *Songs of Praise.*

Ben had been a churchgoer for 72 years, all of his life. He had held many posts of responsibility within the church over the years. When his wife died six years ago he was the churchwarden. The local church had been the main focus of their life together. Over the years Ben had come to detest modern worship; he was a '*Book of Common Prayer* man' and loved the traditional hymns. It was only when his wife died that he stopped going to church. Two years ago he remarried. His second wife has developed dementia. Ben continues to believe totally in God, but has no place for church. Like Charles, Ben welcomes friends from church. Lost but hopefully not forgotten.

We can only imagine the difficulties for an older person in returning to church after many years of absence. The doors must seem like an insurmountable barrier, and where do you sit which will not remind you of your spouse? No wonder *Songs of Praise* is so attractive.

Bereavement of a spouse or partner is dreadful. Maybe we cannot stop people leaving as a consequence, but we can surely continue to visit and keep in touch. Practical gestures such as flowers from church, or little booklets, poems and verses about bereavement and faith to help people through this testing time, are likely to be much appreciated. More importantly, the comfort of a friend or the listening ear of a sensitive bereavement visitor can begin to help make the unbearable bearable.

It is encouraging to learn from our research that, although after the death of a spouse people can leave church for an average of 10 years, many do tend to return. Some of them have appreciated the pastoral ministry that was offered through the funeral visits and funeral service long before. But the lesson for churches is to go on caring for as long as it takes. Peter Brierley wisely comments:

> It is therefore critical not just that there be bereavement counselling and support at the time of death, but specific ongoing friendship and help in the weeks and months afterwards. Otherwise they may be out of church for the next 10 years or more.

In the case of older bereaved people, this may mean for life.


**The role of the minister in pastoral care**
Sensitivity and awareness are so essential in a priest or minister in situations such as those described above, as is the ability to listen and to hear. Those of us who are ministers do well to ask ourselves some searching questions. Are we too busy to listen? Don't we want to get involved? Are older people not our ministry? Are we afraid to face our own death and mortality? Will we share the tasks of pastoral care and bereavement counselling with suitable and trained lay people?

One minister visited a terminally ill man who had been in hospital with dementia for four years. The man had only hours to live and neither the vicar nor other people from the church had ever visited him before, even though he and his wife were members. The minister sat on the spare bed next to the dying man and looked rigidly at the wife, never once allowing his eyes to go to the dying man. The minister was uncomfortable and unable to give any effective care or support.  He socialised for a few minutes and left without giving comfort and without offering prayer.  This minister was in his mid-40s.  The next time they met was at the funeral.  There was a full church, but rarely did anyone visit when the man was alive.

We do well to remind ourselves that ministers too are human.  Whether ordained or not, we are all at times going to let other people down because we are human and vulnerable ourselves.  One elderly vicar woke up to find his wife dead beside him.  He had promised to stand in at a church where there was no one to cover.  With all his training, although he was in profound shock, he got up and went and took the service.  Nobody at that service knew what had happened.  This priest had not visited folk for a long time because he was wrapped up in caring for his wife.  It was very sad.  Ministers are vulnerable too, they have their own journey to make and often their own caring demands at home.

**Summary**
Effective pastoral care will depend on harnessing the gifts and the abilities of the whole church, and being honest about what can and cannot be done.  What you cannot manage to achieve now in pastoral care can be held up in prayer and be remembered before God.  It doesn't help at all for everybody to be running around at full stretch, feeling guilty or worn out.  We have to love one another and help to carry one another's burdens, but we also need to look after ourselves, to be kind to ourselves, to love ourselves, and to forgive ourselves and each other.

An elderly lady, Lily, lived some distance from the church.  She had attended the church for nearly 60 years.  As she became frailer due to infirmity she was unable to get to church any more.  Lily stopped sending her collection envelopes.  At the end of the year she had a letter reminding her that her envelopes were due.  Every year she was asked for her dues.  As the months went by and nobody came to see her, she felt very let down.  As she prepared for her death she was hurt and isolated.  Lily felt that she no longer belonged to the church.  She decided that she wanted to have her funeral at the crematorium not at the church. On Lily's death her daughter rang the minister and asked if he would take the funeral at the local crematorium. He refused, saying that he didn't do crematorium funerals, he didn't believe in them. She should get somebody else. A total stranger did Lily's funeral service. Lily's family made the decision never to put a foot inside a church again.

In Lily's case there was broken fellowship, no belonging, no affirmation, poor pastoral care, monumental insensitivity. Our survey showed that too many older people felt that they could be abandoned by the church. 'I feel, perhaps mistakenly, that I could be abandoned if I was ill for a long time.' 'I feel unwanted,' said another person, 'perhaps they are happier when I am not there.' We need to heed these voices and not just those of contented older people in churches – with whom we rejoice!

Together we are called to be the body of Christ. With God's help and the guidance of the Holy Spirit we need to get our priorities right. We have a mandate to seek out the lost. Jesus told the story of the shepherd with a hundred sheep: 'Which one of you if he lost one, wouldn't leave the 99 to go and search for it?' Wherever possible we are called to seek out those who are lost, lonely and vulnerable. This means that we are to love and nurture all those in our care, and to affirm and empower older people in the church and in the community.

---

**References**
1 Peter Brierley, *UK Christian Handbook Religious Trends 2000-2001*, Christian Research, 2000.
2 Kenneth Howse op. cit. p.69-78.
3 Richter and Francis op. cit. p.121.
4 See Richter and Francis op. cit. pp.127-132.
5 Ibid p.125.
6 Ibid p.124.

7  For information on the Memory Box, contact FIEP Leeds, Leeds Church Institute, 20 New Market Street, Leeds LS1 6DG.

8  Howse op. cit. p.72.

9  Packs concerned with visiting people with dementia are obtainable from FIEP Leeds, CCOA, and Methodist Homes.

10 Andrew Cunnington, *How Can This Be?*, Chichester Diocese, 2000.

11 Information can be obtained from Rev David Cooper, 29 Burlington Road, Altrincham, Cheshire WA14 1HR.

12 Information about Live at Home can be obtained from Methodist Homes.

13 Age Concern England, *Claim to be Heard*, 1980.

14 Howse op. cit. p.55.

15 Richter and Francis op. cit. p.126.

16 Howse op. cit. pp.38-40.

17 Ibid p.40.

18 Ibid p.55.

19 Albert Jewell (ed.), *Spiritual Perspectives on Ageing*, Methodist Homes, 1998, paper E.

20 See Halley Stewart Booklets Nos 7, 9 and 10; also resources available from FIEP Leeds and CCOA.

21 See Jackie Treetops, *A Daisy Among the Dandelions*, FIEP Leeds, 1992, and *Holy, Holy, Holy*, FIEP Leeds 1996.

22 See Halley Stewart Booklet No 6.

# Chapter Four

# WORSHIPPING

## WHAT IS WORSHIP?

The English word 'worship' is derived from 'worth-ship'. In essence it means giving highest place or value to someone or something in one's life. Everything else will fall into place in relationship to that highest value. Of course, the object of worship need not necessarily be the Christian God (or indeed any divine being) but this chapter will restrict itself to that understanding.

If, as the 1647 Shorter Westminster Catechism maintains, the chief end of man is 'to glorify God and to enjoy him for ever', it would seem that worship is something basic to human nature and that it is lifelong – and beyond. Many Christians would argue that worship is the primary purpose of the Church, some would say its only purpose. Church buildings and communities exist to remind people of this basic human need and to provide them with opportunities and liturgies to express that worship together with other believers.

This is not the place to deal at length with the regular contents of worship, from the initial welcome to the final blessing, including hymns and prayers, the reading and exposition of the Bible etc. However, it may be helpful to indicate the dynamics that are at work in most church services as follows:

1. Meeting with God (his presence)
2. Receiving from God (word and sacrament)
3. Sharing with God (prayer)
4. Being changed by God and offering to God (response).

Monica Furlong, in her book *C of E – The State It's In*, approves a similar understanding of the core elements in worship, suggested by David Stancliffe, the Bishop of Salisbury:

1. A sense at the beginning of a service of a gathering of the community
2. Engaging with the Word
3. An experience of transformation
4. 'Sending us out in the power of your Spirit to live and work . . .'[1]

Older people who have been regular churchgoers will have imbibed something of this understanding over the years even if they do not articulate it in such terms. These are the elements they will be expecting to find in worship.

Because worship is a central and regular activity within every kind of Christian community, its potential and purpose are greatly diminished when older people are absent from it. This is a matter of regret when it is caused through physical circumstances, though it is often possible to create alternative and more intimate opportunities, especially for those who are housebound. However, when older people relinquish their churchgoing because they feel marginalised, this is surely tragic both for them and for the congregation from which they have withdrawn. Whereas younger churchgoers may leave one church yet eventually go elsewhere, possibly changing denominations, this is less true of older people who may, therefore, be lost totally to the church. If this happens then the opportunities for sustaining them through teaching and fellowship are also likely to be lost.

## CHANGES IN WORSHIP

Though it would be quite wrong to assume that ageing in itself necessarily leads to nostalgic attitudes to the content of worship, the pace and degree of liturgical change has been most marked in recent decades amongst all denominations. This has certainly made it hard for some older people to make adjustments in an area of their life where they have sought consistency, familiarity and a sense of organisational stability. Removal of or changes to too many trusted landmarks can lead them to feel bewildered and bereft. People seeking to return to church in their later years after long absence may well find little that is recognisable in the worship they encounter.

## 1. Liturgical
Changes in the ethos and content of worship have happened in seemingly opposing directions. On the one hand there has been the creation of a spate of formalised written liturgies and, because of the work of the Joint Liturgical Commission, considerable congruence, for example, in the eucharistic services of many of the main denominations. Within the Free Churches there is much more use of printed orders of service and a greater appreciation of responsive worship and intercessions which involve the congregations.

On the other hand much greater freedom and spontaneity have developed in worship. Within the Roman Catholic Church a quite fundamental change was the vernacularisation of the liturgy after centuries of using Latin as the common language. In the Church of England the *Alternative Service Book*, introduced in 1980 to stand alongside the *Book of Common Prayer* but virtually replacing it, is now giving way to the new book, *Common Worship*. The *Methodist Worship Book* of 1999 illustrates both trends, offering nearly 600 pages of largely formalised services and worship material which is drawn from Methodist and a rich and wide variety of other historical and contemporary Christian sources.

## 2. The Bible
Until 50 years ago the Authorised Version of the Bible was virtually ubiquitous in non-Roman Catholic Churches. The versions by Moffatt, Wearmouth, J B Phillips and others might be referred to by preachers but were rarely read from or made readily available in public worship. From 1950 to 1970 a new era was inaugurated with the publication of the Revised Standard, New English and Jerusalem versions, and nowadays amongst many contenders one is most likely to encounter the Good News

Bible or New International Version in English churches across the Protestant denominations. Such modern versions can offer a clarity and immediacy of the word when used in acts of worship or Bible study. However, for many (especially older) people well-loved and memorised phrases and passages are not easily replaced.

## 3. Music

Although many churches still have their own organists, there are fewer musicians who are competent on this instrument, hence the application of computer technology in producing organs which, with the help of CD discs, have done away with the need for human accompanists. Formal choirs are a thing of the past in many Free Churches where there was a long tradition of anthems and cantatas. Increasingly church worship is served by keyboards and worship groups incorporating vocalists, flutes, drums, guitars and a variety of other instruments. Depending upon the sensitivity and skill of those involved, this can be helpful to express the various moods in worship or produce far too much volume for the liking of many older worshippers.

For some congregations there has been a discovery of the beauty of plainsong and other music from the pre-Reformation period. For others there has been growing appreciation of contemporary poets and hymn-writers such as Brian Wren, Fred Pratt Green and Graham Kendrick who can be most effective in affirming Christian faith in the modern world or focusing on a social gospel. Such hymns have also led to the composition of distinctive new tunes. There has been a burgeoning of music which accords with secular and popular trends, not least through the use of worship songs and choruses. The last 20 years have seen a great volume of new hymn books and musical worship material published by the national churches and by independent publishers. Taizé and Iona have produced their own distinctive words and music which have been widely influential.

Most of the new worship material is available for churches to reproduce and use through the Christian Copyright

Licensing scheme. [2] Many local churches now offer several different hymn and song collections to worshippers who can sometimes be somewhat bewildered by the choices available. Others have virtually dispensed with books and mostly use overhead projection. This enables worshippers to hold their heads up but perhaps benefits the long-sighted rather more than the short-sighted!

It has to be said that *Songs of Praise* on television, and to a lesser extent *Sunday Half-Hour* on radio, have gone some way towards helping their predominantly older audiences to appreciate new words and music within a largely traditional context. At a time of life when such opportunities for participating in worship in one's own home are valued, it is to be hoped that these programmes will not fall prey to the cut-backs that seem to have been a feature of religious broadcasting in recent years. The deletion of familiar programmes or changes to their time-slot or ethos invariably bring a large volume of protest from older viewers and listeners.

## 4. Preaching

The style, content and duration of sermons have altered in response to trends in the media towards approaches that are more visual and pithy and to the view that the average person's concentration span is but a few minutes. If the 'classical' sermon usually contained three points and lasted about 20 minutes, that is no longer the norm. Within the Roman Catholic tradition the relatively brief and focused homily often still obtains and within some Anglican and Free Churches, especially those of an evangelical persuasion, extensive biblical expositions may still be heard. However, many preachers now adopt a more discursive and 'chatty' mode, the teaching can be by dialogue, visual image, or recorded material, and it is not unusual for a church to incorporate within its main worship time for group discussion or Bible study. The preacher is no longer 'six foot above contradiction' and the congregation is no longer content just to sit back and be fed.

## 5. Congregational participation

Until the last 20 or 30 years lay involvement in worship (apart from preachers and organists) was mostly restricted to people fulfilling formal roles as churchwardens, deacons, stewards and sidesmen, or to singing in the choir. Many congregations now involve a large number of people taking a major part in the conduct of services, not least in the music. Lay people of all ages have roles to play in reading lessons and prayers, and in distributing the elements at the Eucharist or Holy Communion. Members of the congregation may be invited to contribute to the intercessions in an extemporary fashion or to write down their concerns on entering church to be incorporated at the appropriate time in the service.

Participation is also more 'physical'. Churches of most denominations have discovered 'the peace' which can be exchanged at Communion; this may be quite restrained or involve members of the congregation to such an extent that they greet everyone in church no matter where they may be sitting! Drama and dance are not infrequently used, usually performed by special groups but sometimes much more spontaneously. In churches of widely differing theological approaches there is now often an emphasis upon healing with the opportunity, either at Communion or otherwise, to receive the laying on of hands, sometimes anointing with oil, and appropriate prayer. The charismatic movement has encouraged people to be freer in the use of their bodies in worship, and in some traditions the utterance of prophecies, speaking in tongues and its interpretation have great potency.

## A CHURCH FOR ALL FAMILY MEMBERS?

One development above all others deserves to be singled out for special consideration because it can lead to older people feeling excluded despite the good intentions that have inspired it.

With the aim of enabling people of all ages to feel at ease and to gain benefit from participating in church services, there have been many attempts over the past 50 years to promote 'family church' or 'all-age worship'. The Sunday school teaching resources found in *Partners in Learning* and some other publications provide thematically-linked material for adults (as well as children) and for use in church services where a wide distribution of ages is present. With a dramatic fall in the number of children attending Sunday schools, calculated by Christian Research at a loss rate of 1,000 per week over the last 10 years,[3] there is an understandable and commendable endeavour to respond to their needs within the main act of worship on Sunday mornings.

In practice, however, inappropriate versions of 'all-age worship' may result, seemingly geared only to making everything accessible to the youngest present rather than ensuring that all age groups and sections of the church can participate and share relevantly. Older people in particular can feel that there is little in such services to satisfy their needs and sustain their faith. Longstanding saints of the Christian life can feel that the essential mystery of worshipping God has been lost.

It is possible to provide satisfactory 'all-age worship' but it does require a great deal of commitment, hard work and the studied and continued effort to include people throughout the age range. Some congregations may in effect choose to go all out for the young, many of whom desire lively and entertaining worship, and make no concession to older people. Churches that seek to be more inclusive may need to ask whether it would be better to provide a mixture of services in different styles, so that people of different ages and temperaments can worship as they wish. Older people, for example, may enjoy *Songs of Praise*, Moody and Sankey or Wesley and Watts services.

The alternative – of trying to please everyone – can end in causing dissatisfaction to all. Richter and Francis comment with insight: 'Perhaps the least successful approach nowadays is to try to blend every cultural taste into a single main worship service, which offers enough of each worship style to alienate its opponents but is insufficient to please its advocates!'[4] If alternative services are seen as the best way forward it is important that there should be other occasions when the whole church family can meet together, perhaps over refreshments between services or by providing other specific opportunities for recreation, learning and social interaction.

The notion and practice of 'all-age worship' may also fall into the trap of not taking sufficient note of those, including many older people, who remain or were once members of the church family but are unable to attend Sunday worship. Solitary worship may take place by choice – but, perhaps more often, because of lack of choice! Isolated older people will feel that they still truly belong if representatives of the church family are able to go to them to conduct informal acts of worship, to celebrate Communion, or to take to them tapes of church services to which they can listen at their personal convenience.

Residents of care homes, whether or not they currently belong to churches, are amongst the most socially excluded members of the community and may have little or no opportunity to take part in services. The sense of isolation and the feeling of being forgotten can be intensified for those who suffer from dementia, as we have seen in earlier chapters. Dementia presents a considerable challenge to achieving 'a church for all family members'. This was recognised in the Church of England report *Ageing* published a decade ago and its comments on inclusiveness bear repetition today:

> Action is needed at the level of local church life to enable those with dementia to be included. This will involve learning to communicate, both in pastoral contact and in worship, in a different way, emphasising the sensual and the present. All those with dementia retain some sensory function. Sight, sound, touch and taste evoke strong responses. It may thus be possible for people with dementia to respond to worship and to respond to the worship of others. Candles, incense, the kiss of peace, the feel of the cross, the taste of

bread and wine, familiar word-patterns in prayer and music, especially hymns, become more significant than the words of liturgy or sermon.[5]

Even when church attendance is not possible:

They must be found a place within the body of Christ . . . when individual identity is collapsing the members of the body of Christ can uphold that person and those who love them in the hope of the resurrection.[6]

## OUR RESEARCH

Granted that people with dementia do not have much opportunity to communicate their views, how far did our investigations discover that older people feel dissatisfied with their experience of church worship or marginalised by the liturgical changes that have taken place in recent years?

In the focus groups it proved easy to get those attending to talk about worship which was obviously a matter close to their hearts. 'Church' to most of them equated with their place of worship. However, as might be expected, their responses were very diverse and at times contradictory. Temperamentally, and in terms of their personal expectations of worship, older people demonstrate as wide a variety of views as people of other age groups. Secondary analysis of the considerable data amassed by Francis and Richter reveals the same breadth of opinion with regard to the formal and the informal, the traditional and the modern.

In the preliminary questionnaires completed by those attending the focus groups those still attending church (some 49) were asked to identify the two things they liked best about it. Thirty-three pointed to fellowship and friendship, 26 to worship or particular aspects of worship. No other category scored more than 3. Conversely, the things they least liked included long boring sermons (6 in number) and new hymns (3 in number) but only one each highlighted such matters as intrusive music and new translations of the Bible. Indeed, there were six people who deprecated their church for being unwilling to try new things! Interestingly, the highest response in relation to a question about changing one thing in the Church in this country was that there should be more frequent ecumenical services.

At the actual group meetings these areas were explored further. When those who did still go to church were asked their main reason for doing so, 17 (out of some 40) replied that it was in order to worship. Fourteen indicated that it was for friendship and company. They were also asked what were the most important needs they felt were met by going to church. Here 22 identfied worship and the same number fellowship.

Four aspects of worship were then suggested as being important. The outcome for churchgoers showed that hymns (25), a sense of the presence of God (23) and prayers (22) were rated highest, with sermons a rather poor fourth at 17. The responses from non-churchgoers were similar, with some outspoken criticism of modern hymns and songs but with no takers for the presence of God.

Miscellaneous comments in our investigations reveal that some unhappiness was felt concerning what is nowadays included in or excluded from worship: 'Standing too long for never-ending choruses'; 'Mass is over so quickly . . . I like it slow and contemplative'; 'Being asked to come forward to the Lord. Don't they know we have a faith – done it all before'; 'A conspiracy of silence in sharing theological problems'; 'Too many gimmicks'. Such cries from the heart do evidence some sense of marginalisation on the part of older worshippers.

Our quantitative research to a large degree confirmed the evidence produced by the focus groups and also added interesting information. Of those who had at some stage stopped attending church, only 1% attributed it to dull church services; overwhelmingly the reasons given had to do with changed personal circumstances. Eighty-five per cent of all the churchgoers found their deepest sense of God's closeness in church services. However, 60% of all respondents also mentioned outdoors in a garden or the countryside. Peter Brierley comments: 'The saying "you are nearer God's heart in a garden than anywhere else on earth" perhaps has a special echo for elderly people.' Anecdotal evidence certainly seems to confirm that older people develop a special appreciation of the world of nature and of the seasons which may be related to the conscious or unconscious acknowledgement that there may be rather fewer years of life ahead. Listening to music (apart from church worship) was also important to 36% of respondents.

The most important sources of spiritual nourishment reported by church and non-churchgoers combined were church services (76%), hymns and songs (73%) and prayer (57%). Virtually 80% of all respondents claimed to pray daily, and of those the vast majority prayed mostly for friends and family, followed by thanksgiving to God, healing for particular people, suffering in the world and strength for the day. Affirming older people should surely include acknowledging these concerns in public worship and ensuring that devotional resources produced for those staying at home take account of these essential areas.

The questionnaire also asked what single change recipients would like to make in the local church in order to encourage older people more. A third of churchgoers and a fifth of non-churchgoers responded. Eighty per cent of them were concerned with physical changes to improve accessibility or with church services themselves. Of the latter some wanted more sensible service times on Sundays and during the week, others wanted more traditional and fewer 'modern' services. More strikingly some urged that the church should be protected as a place of peace not noise and others asked to be allowed to choose the hymns sometimes – which seems a rather modest request!

## WIDER ENDORSEMENT

The question that now remains to be addressed is how far the rather disparate findings of our research are confirmed or contradicted by the reflections of other recent writers who have concerned themselves with older people and church worship. What are the main points in their diagnosis and how may they help churches wishing to address this important area? Suggestions will be made after each section for possible use with a church council or appropriate church group.

### Pace of change

It is recognised that change in worship is a particularly sensitive matter and needs to be approached accordingly, wherever possible with proper consultation, the honest facing of pros and cons and an openness to compromise. Richter and Francis wisely comment: 'As far as possible, churches need to avoid manoeuvring people into tight corners, from which the only way of saving face is to leave the church.'[7]

The problem is, of course, that preferred styles of worship are very much a matter of personal taste. Richter and Francis found in their research that of those who left church later in life as many did so complaining that worship was too formal as did complaining that it was too informal.

*Suggestion*
The following might be a useful exercise for church leaders to engage in with their core congregation:

- To identify the main changes in worship in that church over the past 20 years
- To rehearse the reasons for those changes
- To decide how helpful or off-putting those changes have been for older worshippers and for others.

### A sense of God's presence

If the essence of worship is to meet with God, those attending worship need to find some sense of his presence. This is something that many of our respondents sought to articulate. In the case of those who expressed disaffection on this score the implication must be that much worship is too busy or noisy, too wordy or too human-centred, to facilitate this sense of the presence of God. Richter and Francis found that one in four of all their respondents, of whatever age group, attributed their leaving church at least in part to finding too little of that presence in church services.[8]

Christopher Burkett, an Anglican priest who is a diocesan ministry review officer, in the publication *Leading, Managing, Ministering* quotes David Bosch:

> People do not only need truth and justice, they also need beauty, the rich resources of symbol, piety, worship, love, awe and mystery.[9]

These are dimensions not always present in much modern worship.

As a result of what his older parishioners had shared with him, Andrew Cunnington urged that:

> Worship is no longer directed to a God we think we have fully fathomed out, or who will only accept that worship if all proper rubrics have been observed, but space needs to be given amidst the sharing of Word and the Sacrament for each person to contemplate the mystery and celebrate the journey they are on and to find inspiration for the next step.[10]

*Suggestion*
Discuss with an older people's group in the church or a mixed-age group what are the things that enhance their sense of God's presence and what are the things that detract from it.

What can be done to meet legitimate criticisms?

**Cultural division**
In his Help the Aged lecture, 'Maturity for Beginners – The Church and an Ageing Population', the Moderator of the Free Church Council, Rev Anthony Burnham, reflecting on

relationships between young and old people, suggests that in worship, as in the whole of church life, there are profound cultural considerations, such as the differences in musical taste of people of different generations and contrasting patterns of educational development. This means that

> a congregation of largely elderly people, no matter how active, perpetuates a style of church life that is increasingly out of touch with younger people.

This can be most pronounced in regard to the timing and content of church worship. He urges the need to create space and opportunity for the younger generations. The assumption appears to be that, if concessions are to be made or generosity exercised, this should be on the part of older church members.[11]

Christopher Burkett takes the cultural aspect of worship equally seriously but draws a rather different conclusion. He recognises that all worship takes place within a cultural framework. Its aim is the worship of God but its social function is to create a common sense of identity and to reinforce shared beliefs and values. If that social function is damaged it becomes easier for a person to leave the congregation.[12] This is perhaps why people can appear to be so 'touchy' about changes in worship. In fact, in the current discussion of numerical decline in churches, he maintains that being a member of a congregation has held up better than many types of belonging in other voluntary organisations. However, a high degree of sensitivity and responsibility is called for on the part of those who, within their own tradition, are called to exercise leadership, especially in relation to worship. A whole value base and way of life is sustained by a shared pattern of worship. Once dismantled or radically changed, worship will no longer nurture and sustain the lives of those who feel that they and their needs have been marginalised.

*Suggestion*
There is material for a profound discussion about the cultural aspects of worship at a church meeting or council:

- The liturgies of the Orthodox Churches have changed very slowly over many centuries and still have the power to attract millions of people of all ages. Why is this so?

- Very modern 'alternative worship' employing a multi-media approach can attract and retain lots of young people. What is the secret of its success?

- Can old and young in your church honestly share together what they are really seeking in worship and how far they find it?

- In her lively book, *C of E – The State It's In*, Monica Furlong says of patterns of worship that: 'The loss of the old, though painful, makes room for new kinds of creativity.'[13] How far does your church believe this to be true?

## Getting real

In one sense worship enables those involved to enter into another world, to find a door opening for a brief while into heaven, to recapture a vision of the Kingdom of God. It may, therefore, appear to be illusory to some or to be escapist from the real world. Nearly 42% of the older church leavers identified by secondary analysis of the Richter and Francis data believed that the church failed to connect with the rest of life (though this was not solely related to worship). The response may well be given that worshippers are helped to focus on the one reality against which every other must be measured, an ultimate reality which renews the commitment and sense of purpose of those who worship. However, the actual experience may fall far short of the ideal.

In the course of our investigations we have found a significant number of older people who feel that much modern worship is indeed escapist and thus not helpful to those who wish to work out the purposes of God in the real world. They speak of empty worship songs, sentimentalism, and sermons that seek to give false reassurance which flies in the face of the realities of life. Such teaching lacks substance and fibre. Richter and Francis go so far as to say:

> If a church's teachings, however impressive they may be, fail to enable people to engage their faith with their everyday life, with its hopes and fears, successes and failures, the church itself may eventually be discarded as 'irrelevant'.[14]

Such sadly would appear to have been the verdict of many former churchgoers. Secondary analysis shows that a third of the Richter and Francis respondents aged over 60 reported that they had found sermons irrelevant to their lives.

In the cause of better intergenerational understanding Anthony Burnham issues a challenge to the churches which, if responded to positively, would also help to answer the disaffection of such thinking and concerned older people. He maintains that churches need 'to make a radical switch of educational resources from the younger to the older generations', with teaching that responds to 'the questions and dilemmas of life experience'. He adds the shrewd comment:

> Education, apart from that which is vocational, is better given when the pupils are ready and eager to learn. Ageing provides both time and motive.[15]

Many older people we have met during the course of our investigations would say 'Amen' to that!

### Suggestion

Ask members of the congregation to monitor worship and preaching over a given period such as a month, noting the occasions when issues that are real for them or in the wider world were dealt with or prayed about. The results can be shared with each other (and the local minister) at a meeting.

## A POSITIVE POSTSCRIPT

It has been suggested that worship is the most important activity of any church and a touchstone of that church's relevance to the lives of its members and local community.

'I'm afraid that ours is an ageing congregation.' Must this always be interpreted in a negative manner? Does it necessarily imply decline in the vibrancy and vision of that congregation? The following example, which is not untypical of such churches, shows that there are still some signs of hope and of lively Christian outreach.

In one district of a northern town a large local chapel was demolished as part of a local process of urban regeneration. In its place specialised residential units were built alongside a smaller replacement church capable of use for worship and community activities. The local community is now a place of differing faiths and cultures, many members of which use and benefit from this church's resources.

The church shares a minister with two other congregations so, not uncommonly within Non-conformist congregations, lay leadership is critical. In this, the role of the Church Meeting in decision-making is important. As in almost all denominations, so is a shared responsibility for sustaining the weekly programme of worship and activities and maintaining an attractive building.

A Sunday morning service is likely to be attended by 40 or 50 people but the church community is probably twice that number. There are a dozen or so children and some young middle-aged, but the church is predominantly made up of old people, many of them over 75. To attend an act of worship in this 'ageing congregation' is to be made aware of a strength of Christian faith and, in their case, of a positive acceptance of contemporary words and music. There is evidence, on the walls and over the coffee counter, of commitment to world issues – social, economic and environmental. Here are links with Christians in other countries. Nearer to home the church enables the minister to spend much time, pastorally and educationally, in responding to the needs of substantial numbers of asylum seekers who have been sent to the town. They too use the premises.

Many of the older people continue to provide creative leadership and to offer generously of their time, talents and money. Will it last? Can it last? It exists – here and now! These older people do not feel marginalised or disadvantaged. They are by no means on the margins of the church's life. They are its central resource.

## References

1　Monica Furlong, *C of E – The State It's In*, Hodder and Stoughton, 1999, p.318.

2　Christian Copyright Licensing (Europe) Ltd, 26 Gildridge Road, Eastbourne BN21 4SA.

3　Peter Brierley, *The Tide is Running Out*, Christian Research, 2000, ch. 4.

4　Richter and Francis, op. cit. p.150.

5　*Ageing*, Church House Publishing, 1990, p.93.

6　Ibid p.94.

7　Richter and Francis op. cit. p.162.

8　Ibid p.116.

9　Christopher Burkett, *Leading, Managing, Ministering* (ed John Nelson, Canterbury Press, 1999, p.217, quoting David Bosch, *Transforming Mission*, Orbit, New York, 1991.

10　Andrew Cunnington, *How Can This Be?*, Chichester Diocese, 2000.

11　Anthony Burnham, *Maturity for Beginners*, Cecil Jackson-Cole Memorial Lecture, Help the Aged, 1999.

12　Christopher Burkitt op. cit. p. 205f.

13　Monica Furlong op. cit.

14　Richter and Francis op. cit. p.114.

15　Anthony Burnham op. cit.

# Chapter Five

# BELIEVING

The year 2000 brought the publication of two pieces of research that are directly relevant to our own but which, on the surface at least, are strangely conflicting in their findings. The outcome of the English Church Attendance Survey for 1998 [1] carried out by Christian Research revealed disastrous drops in church attendance over the previous decade in every age group except the over 65s. These had dropped 9% in the 1980s but recovered in the 1990s adding 4% to their number. Comparing the actual loss in this age group in churches with the much higher death rate in the population at large during the same period, Dr Peter Brierley comments that it either means 'that churchgoers live longer than non-churchgoers (which could well be true since many neither smoke nor drink alcohol excessively) or that there has been a substantial influx of older people into churches in the 1990s (which could also well be true with many churches involved with luncheon clubs for the elderly etc).'

On the other hand the longitudinal study of 340 people over 65 in Southampton carried out by Professor Peter Coleman [2] shows a progressive decline in religious allegiance over a 20 year period from 1977. Of those interviewed after the first 10 years of the programme 26% said that religion now meant less to them than before, with only 3% claiming the opposite. By 1993 these figures had become 37% and 9% respectively. Some caution may be called for in that the ever increasing number of deaths over the years has reduced considerably the number of participants in this study and may have led to some distortion in the results. However, such findings may be seen to confirm the judgement of Richter and Francis: 'Church leaving is typically gradual and involves a period during which a person's religious identity, lifestyle and understanding of the world is re-evaluated.' [3] Their full statistical data also show that loss of faith is given as a reason for leaving church by nearly a third of all respondents, amongst whom the highest proportion is of people currently aged over 60 (though, of course, the data does not reveal at what age they lost their faith).

That part of our own quantitative survey concerned with faith offered five basic touchstones of Christian belief: that God created the world, that God is a God of love, that Jesus Christ was more than just a man, that he rose from the dead, and that God can influence my life today. Churchgoing respondents reported that they believed strongly or most of the time at levels of between 77% (Creator God) and 91% (God's influence today). The non-churchgoers responded proportionately, varying between 50% and 60% as between the same two categories. Perhaps even more surprisingly, 85% of the churchgoers and 65% of the non-churchgoers said that they prayed daily. Indeed, only 5% of the latter declared that they 'hardly ever' prayed.

What are we to make of these contrasting outcomes? Were the respondents to our questionnaire less than honest in giving the answers they perhaps thought might be expected of them? Were Peter Coleman's interviewees more candid because they were involved in the research over such a long time period? Certainly the findings of such longitudinal and in-depth research need to be carefully heeded. Were those reasonably happy within the Christian fellowship (whom we tended to access) more disposed to overlook faith questions or take the answers for granted? If it is true that the nearer approach of death concentrates people's minds on spiritual matters, were our respondents amongst the more healthy and active segments of the Christian community? It is not easy to suggest answers.

However, it is likely that Professor Coleman has put his finger on trends towards a lessening in Christian belief and church adherence which will certainly be working its way through successive generations of ageing people and to which the Christian community needs to be alert. He comments: 'At the very least our findings suggest that churches should not take the allegiance of their older members for granted, that faith is not a given at this stage of life.' Those reaching old age in the 21st century are progressively less likely to have been exposed to the influence of Sunday school, church and religious education in schools than their predecessors. In future progressively fewer ageing people will have Christian roots to which to return. The great and continuing reduction in younger people attending all mainstream Christian churches noted by Peter Brierley can only intensify the trend as in due course they pass up the demographic ladder.

Moreover we have experienced a scientific and technological revolution that in many ways may be seen to challenge religious faith. People growing older today are likely to have been educated into a more secular outlook. They live in a society which encourages personal choice and there are many forms of spirituality to choose from other than the mainstream Christian traditions. We shall examine these and other contributory factors later in this chapter.

## THE MEANING OF LIFE

Many very old people find themselves saying things like: 'I can't see any purpose in going on. What's the point?' What they are expressing is both a conscious weariness with their own existence and also the underlying human need to find if life does in fact have any ultimate meaning. Is there a purpose, a wider and deeper context into which our life on earth fits? Are there grounds for believing that the whole story is not told within the span of our 70 or 80 years on earth? Is there life beyond which brings to fulfilment all that we have striven to be and hoped for and makes sense of it all?

Do we believe that as human beings we are just the product of blind biological forces, that our life has no ultimate meaning, and that physical death is the end of everything? Or do we believe that there is another world, the world of a Creator God, that is not limited to this world of time and space?

The agnostic philosopher Bertrand Russell, in his book, *Mysticism and Logic,* [4] describes what this first alternative means:

That Man is the product of causes which had no prevision of the end they were achieving; that his origin, his growth, his hopes and fears, his loves and beliefs, are but the outcome of accidental collocations of atoms; that no fire, no heroism, no intensity of thought and feeling, can preserve an individual life beyond the grave; that all the labours of the ages, all the devotion, all the inspiration, all the noonday brightness of human genius, are destined to extinction in the vast death of the solar system, and that the whole temple of Man's achievement must inevitably be buried beneath the debris of a universe in ruins – all these things, if not quite beyond dispute, are yet so nearly certain, that no philosophy which rejects them can hope to stand. Only within the scaffolding of these truths, only on the firm foundation of unyielding despair, can the soul's habitation henceforth be safely built.

If a person takes that as his understanding of human life on this planet, there is little room for belief in God or that our lives have any eternal dimension.

This view does not, of course, mean that we cannot as a member of the human family offer service to others, or that we simply turn away from causes which claim the sacrifice of time and effort. Bertrand Russell himself will long be remembered for his concern to rid the world of nuclear weapons as in his 80s and 90s he was at the front of the nuclear disarmament marches from Aldermaston. We may share the views of Bertrand Russell and still love poetry, listen to great music, make the most of life while we have it, but ultimately we may think life has no meaning other than that which we give it.

An alternative has been described recently by Keith Ward, the Regius Professor of Divinity in the University of Oxford, in his book, *God, Faith and the New Millennium.* [5] 'The Christian view is that one of the chief goals of creation and evolution is the emergence of beings that to some extent possess awareness, creative agency, and powers of reactive and responsible relationship, with whom God can enter into personal fellowship. The universe is ordered from its beginning to the actualisation of beings "made in the image of the Creator".' Human beings, in this view, are not accidental by-products of blind cosmic processes. They are parts of the planned and pre-destined goal of the evolutionary process.

In his book, *The Mind of God*, a mathematical physicist, Professor Paul Davies, wrote: 'I cannot believe that our existence in this universe is a mere quirk of fate, an accident of history, an incidental blip in the great cosmic drama . . . the existence of mind in some organism on some planet is surely a fact of fundamental significance. Through conscious beings, the universe has generated self-awareness. This can be no trivial detail, no minor product of mindless, purposeless forces. We are truly meant to be here.' [6] It follows from this view that human lives which 'express loving dependence on the Father, patterned on and united in Christ, and filled with and shaped by the Spirit . . . can begin to share in the divine nature, and thus foreshadow the destiny that awaits every created personal life'.[7]

Bertrand Russell and Keith Ward reached radically different answers as to the meaning or otherwise of human life on earth. Insofar as they are able to grasp such philosophical language, some people will claim that they have views that are very close to one or the other. Most, however, stand somewhere in the middle and could not express in clear or precise terms what they really believe. Many people believe that there must be a meaning in existence somewhere, but they don't know what it is. Older people, knowing that death is nearer, certainly agonise over what the purpose of their life has been.

## BELIEVING WITHOUT BELONGING

One of Professor Coleman's suggestions from his research is that, although so many people have ceased to feel themselves members of the Christian churches, this does not mean that they have necessarily lost spiritual beliefs or no longer have spiritual needs.

This is a theme developed by Dr Grace Davie, a lecturer in the University of Exeter, who in 1994 published a book with the title *Religion in Modern Britain; Believing without Belonging.*[8] She was intrigued by the persistence of what she called 'unchurched' religion in Britain. In a more recent article in *Epworth Review* in April 2000, she identified a number of significant events in the closing years of the 20th century which provoked – or were provoked by – an unexpected religious response and associated debate. She pointed to the death of 95 Liverpool football fans at Hillsborough football ground in Sheffield in April 1989; the killing of 16 young schoolchildren at Dunblane in 1996; the death of Princess Diana in a car accident in Paris in August 1997; the sacking of Glen Hoddle as the England football coach in February 1999 following his remarks on the possible reasons why certain people suffer a disability; and the dismay of the secular media at the popularity of Cliff Richard's record of the Lord's Prayer set to the tune of 'Auld Lang Syne' as a Millennium Prayer.[9]

In each case, large numbers of people (young and old) found that religion provided the only context within which they could come to terms with these events. There were still lots of questions left in their minds, but many felt that somewhere in the context of Christian worship and thinking there lay meaning which could bring a sense of peace. This led in turn to the judgement that a growing number of British people have lost their mooring in the institutional churches, but not their inclination to believe. However, Dr Davie writes that the result is that religious belief has become 'individualised, detached, undisciplined and hetero-geneous'. This is so not just for young people but increasingly for older people too.

It seems, therefore, that in Britain today a large proportion of ageing people recognise the importance of spiritual questions, but are not sure where they stand and do not feel the need to belong to a church or religious group in which they can develop their spiritual awareness. Our own research found little antagonism to the Church but also that nearly half of those attending church had left at some earlier stage in their life for at least a year. The average age at which this happened was 29 for churchgoers and 34 for non-churchgoers. Two-thirds of the people questioned had stayed away for up to 10 years. Similar evidence was found in the Churches Together '94 Research Project, published as *Finding Faith in 1994*.[10] It is perhaps not surprising that they are in this position, and that Peter Coleman has produced such significant findings, given the changes which have taken place in society and in popular culture during the last century and which continue at such a rapid pace.

## SOME FACTORS IN MODERN SOCIETY

There are at least five factors that interrelate and may well lead to the uncertainty of ageing persons.

### Science and the Bible

The first comes from the difficulty of trying to relate the theories of modern science to the Bible. Many older people went to a Church school or to Sunday school and were taught to think of the Bible as the Word of God. The Bible, they learned, is a book which comes to us from God and God speaks to us through it. They memorised passages from the Bible that they have never forgotten and which comfort them at critical times in life. The Lord's Prayer, the 23rd Psalm, parables like the Good Samaritan and the Prodigal Son, the words of Jesus, 'In my Father's house are many mansions', and the Beatitudes are examples.

In school assemblies and in church and Sunday school worship, they learned some of the great hymns of the Church whose words they recall. Our quantitative research found that 87% of ageing people watch *Songs of Praise* on television – and they are equally divided between church-goers and non-churchgoers. However, there is a dichotomy here, for when they watch programmes on TV like Patrick Moore's *The Sky at Night*, the documentaries of David Attenborough and others on the natural world, or listen to Stephen Hawking, the eminent Cambridge mathematician, they are presented with a view of the world which is very different from the two creation stories at the beginning of Genesis.

Though not all scientists are in agreement, modern science, on the other hand, tells us of a vast universe, some 12 thousand million years old, which began with a Big Bang (or an immense infusion of energy into a small ball of matter) and which has now expanded to consist of thousands of millions of stars arranged in galaxies. The nature programmes are built on a theory that life has evolved over vast stretches of time which accounts for the many different species of plants, birds and animals. And programmes like those of Professor Robert Winston about the way human life began and how it develops as it does give us a very different picture from that of the creation of Adam and Eve from the dust of the earth. Many people, perhaps especially older people, are left bewildered, unsure what to think or believe. Science has transformed the way we live. Has it totally discredited the Bible? Has it now left behind any need to believe in God? Are there reasons still to believe in a Creator? Does a process of evolution by natural selection do away with the need to believe in God? It is significant that almost half of older church leavers identified by secondary analysis of data from the Richter and Francis study had difficulties reconciling faith with modern science.

## Secularism

The second difficulty comes from the fact that in Europe, we live in a secular age, in which religion is pushed to the margins. Secularism is a thesis that arose in Europe. It argues that as Europe's economic and political life developed, dating approximately from the middle of the 18th century, so the place of religion began to diminish in public significance. Personal religion still continued, but increasingly it became a private matter. [11] Over the years, the thesis became ever more widely accepted and was assumed to be a fact. As economic factors continue to change society, and as basic political and moral questions are taken up in all sections of society, so it is assumed by many that religion will just wither away. Hence the decline in church affiliation. And what Europe does today, the rest of the world will do tomorrow.

We can see this thesis being worked out in many sectors of our society. In radio and television, there is now no place as of right for religion. It features only when it is newsworthy.

In debating the answers to ethical questions, of what is right and wrong in human conduct, religion no longer has a dominant voice. That position now goes to the secular expert. Secularism also believes that religion has no place in civil affairs. So in matters of industry, commerce and finance, the standards by which everything is judged are not those of Christianity, but rather those of the market and of profitability. Important decisions are taken because they are good for shareholders, and little consideration may be given to the impact of those decisions upon the men and women and their families who are most affected. In entertainment, in novels, plays and films, Christian moral standards are set aside. The breakdown of marriage and the family is studied from a sociological standpoint, for Christian ethical teaching no longer holds sway. When there is a disaster, the skills of counsellors are judged necessary rather than those of the priest or clergyman.

Are we, then, now living in a post-Christian society, one in which traditional Christian teaching must be left behind, so that by using human reason we can create the kind of society which enables us to do whatever seems best for the human race, or for our part of it? Such matters are deeply disturbing for many older people who believed that Christian moral standards were absolute. The interesting thing is that although the United States has faced the same kind of pressures, religion there is still widely accepted in national and personal life.

**Wars and disasters**
The third difficulty comes from the experience of the world in the last century. In the first half of that century, Britain was involved in a colonial war, the Boer War, followed by two world wars, in 1914-1918 and 1939-1945. Those who fought in those wars witnessed terrible things which scarred their lives. They saw death, suffering and destruction on a vast scale. In the first world war some 13 million people died, many of them still in their teens. The culmination of the second world war was the dropping of the first two atomic bombs on Hiroshima and Nagasaki. Many argue for a direct connection between the experience of men in the

armed forces during these wars and the loss of menfolk from the churches in the UK in the 20th century.

The next 30 years saw Europe divided by the Iron Curtain behind which East and West developed ever more terrible weapons. The horrors of the Holocaust were followed by the Gulag camps of the Soviet Union under Stalin. In many lands, terrible civil wars were fought in which genocide on a vast scale was practised. And all this killing and suffering, added to the awareness that half of the world's population lived in absolute poverty, raised the disturbing question in the minds of all thinking people: why does a God of love, if such a God exists, allow it? Older people have witnessed many of these things during their own lifetimes and they are deeply disturbing to faith, especially when there is added in their personal experience of cancer, bereavement of loved ones and the other trauma that advancing years tend to bring. Richter and Francis refer to John Finney's finding that bereavement and suffering are amongst the significant factors in people becoming a Christian and pertinently comment: 'Equally, sadly, such experiences can lead to loss of faith.'[12]

## Women in society

A fourth issue arises from the greatly changed attitude to the position of women in our society. The development of labour-saving devices has liberated women from the drudgery of housework. Family planning has given them the opportunity to decide how best to plan their lives. So the movement for equal treatment of women in society, which began with the demand for voting rights, has grown to a position when equality in all aspects of life is now seen as right and just. But sections of the Church have resisted the pace of this change that seeks to give women control over their own lives and an equal status in the Church, as in the rest of society. It has been deeply disorientating for some older people.

## Personal choice

The fifth factor is that we now live in a society that is increasingly dominated by personal choice and consumption and by an emphasis on the rights of individuals. The days in which regions of the country took pride in the products of local industry, and felt part of a community to which they made their contribution, lie in the past. Now the emphasis is upon persuading people that the key to a good life lies in the abundance of things they possess. Advertising tells us what is on offer and tries to convince everyone they should possess it or take advantage of it.

And this has had a profound effect upon the life of the Church as well as other sectors of society. When moving, people now tend to change denominational loyalties to choose a church they like. If they don't feel that church worship meets their needs, they don't need to continue going. The positive side of this is that people who attend church do not do so because it is the accepted thing, but because they actually want to go. Probably the level of commitment is greater even though the numbers attending have declined.

A more significant aspect is that in our multi-faith society religious choices are not confined within the broad Christian tradition. People can quite easily explore Eastern religions and a whole variety of spiritualities. Half of all the older respondents identified by secondary analysis of data from the Francis and Richter research attributed the loosening of their church connection to an awareness of other ways of thinking and the belief that all the great religions can be regarded as equally true. The emphasis tends to be upon personal spiritual fulfilment and development rather than community values, and more and more people sample in turn the different alternatives that are on offer or adopt a 'pick and mix' approach. The Christian faith is clearly only one contender for the commitment of the citizens of the UK, including, of course, its senior citizens.

## A NEW APOLOGETIC

So we return to the situation of people ageing in the first years of the 21$^{st}$ century, poised somewhere between the views of Bertrand Russell and Keith Ward, trying to make sense of it all. Those who are in their later years have lived and continue to live through these processes in a society that sends out confused signals. No longer is there the certainty of former centuries when people knew what they believed and how they should behave.

If what we have identified above are some of the major challenges to faith that have arisen during the past century, then it behoves the Christian Church to 'read the changing signs of the times', as Clifford Longley asserted, writing in the *Daily Telegraph* of 14 January 2000. This will require re-visiting and rehabilitating or redefining some of the basics of the faith for the benefit of people of all ages who are bewildered or less sure of their beliefs than once was the case. Indeed, nothing less than a new Christian apologetic is needed which takes us beyond the scope of this book. There is space here only to identify what are perhaps the three most fundamental matters that Christian thinkers are or should be addressing and to give some pointers. However, it is very important that this thinking penetrates into local churches and reaches individual believers or seekers.

## Is there a God?

This question is, of course, the most fundamental of all and quite literally the ultimate one for older people aware of their mortality. We have to accept the fact that the Church cannot now prove the existence of God. In past ages it was believed that convincing reasons could be provided for believing in God's existence, but many scientists and philosophers in the last two centuries have concluded on the basis of their studies and reflection that there is no God. Replies to their views have been provided by thinkers like Hans Küng in his weighty book, *Does God Exist?* [13]

Most Christian scholars would now hold that no single convincing argument for believing that God exists can be advanced but there are many indicators which, taken together, provide reasonable grounds for believing in God. Such grounds include the very persistence of such a belief throughout human history and the equally persistent sense that there is purpose and meaning in this world and in every individual human life. There would also appear to be in every human heart a sense of wonder which many people translate into the activity of worship, giving ultimate value to something or someone beyond themselves. The vast modern expansion of human knowledge can lead to an overreaching hubris of the part of humankind but it can also set the idea of God as Creator within the context of an immense universe, to be understood as creation unfolding through thousands of millions of years.

One of the difficulties many people have is trying to understand what is meant when the Christian creeds speak of God as 'Almighty', and this may be reflected in the findings from our questionnaire that more older people were prepared to accept that God is a God of love than that he is to be seen as Creator. If God is able to do everything, why does he allow so many cruel and unjust things to happen? Jesus may have healed the sick but prayer for sick people today often seems to be unanswered. And what of the victims of earthquakes, famines, floods and other natural disasters?

Any attempted answer to the problem of human suffering will need to address such matters as what we understand to be 'the laws' of the universe, what we mean by 'miracles', what responsibility human beings have for causing or failing to avert such suffering, and not least whether our view of life is limited to this terrestrial one. Christians would want to point to the 'salvation' that is to be found in Christ: forgiveness, 'wholeness' that may not include actual physical healing, and an eternal hope. Most important of all, individuals who suffer are not so much seeking intellectual answers but rather the love, understanding and support that will enable them to bear it even when they cannot possibly understand it. Such love is also very much in the character of Christ. It underlines the imperative nature of the Church's pastoral care.

### What is the Bible?
The Church certainly needs to define what it understands by the description of the Bible as 'the Word of God'. As we have noted, many older people will have been brought up to accept without question that what the Bible says can be accepted as true but then find this understanding to be in conflict with modern thinking and their own experience of

life. In an article entitled 'The Authority of the Bible' the late Archbishop Ramsey wrote: 'It would be wrong to infer from the exalted place of the Bible in every form of Christianity that Christianity is the religion of a Book. The central fact of Christianity is not a Book but a Person – Jesus Christ, himself described as the Word of God.' Our quest is not for an infallible set of ideas or creeds; rather it is for a Person, for God, who Christians believe has revealed himself in Jesus Christ. And a person is much more accessible than a creed.

The Bible, which records in various kinds of literature the human experience of God over a period approaching 2,000 years, can guide us in our quest for God and point us to Jesus. Most Christians do not read the creation stories of Genesis as scientific accounts but those accounts do underline 'truths' of our human relationship and responsibility to God which resonate still today. The story of the Garden of Eden tells us that, whilst we have been given free will, there are limits to our use of this freedom if we want to enjoy an earthly paradise. When we break those limits, we must suffer the consequences. These consequences multiply. If Lamech can take revenge by killing 'seventy times seven', and not just seven as in the case of Cain (Genesis 4:24), in the 20th century one atomic bomb killed 100,000 civilians and the United Nations tells us that in 1992 there were 32 wars in different parts of the world. Ageing people will have lived through much of this.

As we reflect on passages in the Bible, we see how they speak to the minds and hearts of people as the 21st century begins. John Calvin, the Reformer, called the Book of Psalms 'An anatomy of all parts of the Human Soul' because he found within it were mirrored all the problems and emotions of human life. There are Psalms which speak of the human need for God, of people who feel forsaken by God, of individuals in distress crying out for God, of thanksgiving, faith, worship, confidence. Many older people testify to the value of the Psalms and their relevance to their own situation; they express all the basic cries from the human heart. The Bible as a whole, read with understanding and intelligence, reflects life as we still experience it. The Old Testament prepares us for the Good News of the new way opened up for us in Christ, and the New Testament introduces us to his life and continuing impact.

But how is the Bible presented in our churches today? As an infallible book, a blueprint for life, or as holding a mirror up to life – a mirror which also reflects the person of Jesus who is himself the image of God?

### Is there life after death?

This is a question of importance to everyone but is perhaps most pressing for older people. Is there anything beyond this life, and if so will they meet their loved ones again? The one certain fact for those of us in our later years to accept is that our life on earth will end. We know through experience that our friends and loved ones die and so the number of people belonging to our generation declines. Across the world and in most religions, members of the human family have believed that there is life after death. Can we believe that that is true in any more personal way than that we pass on a genetic heritage to our children and grandchildren in this world?

For Christians the real issue is whether or not we believe in the faithfulness and love of God. When someone we love dies, we don't forget them as if they had never existed. Our love for them continues and their memory lives on in our hearts and minds. They continue to touch our lives in all sorts of ways. If God our Creator really loves us – a belief that lies at the heart of the Christian Gospel – then he surely cannot treat us as if all our living and striving on earth has no lasting significance. The Apostle Paul in his great 'hymn to love' says: 'Love never ends'; in this world we never know the full truth but then I will know fully, even as I have been fully known' (I Cor 13: 8,12).

Christians do not claim to have an immortal soul that never dies. The Christian hope is not that we shall survive death because we have a spiritual component that is immortal. It is a belief in death and resurrection. Jesus demonstrates what this means. On the cross he died: his heart ceased beating, the flow of blood to his brain ceased, he stopped breathing. Those who loved him laid him in a tomb. But the clear testimony of the disciples and of the early Church is that Jesus was raised from the dead. He appeared to his followers again and again.

The Christian hope of resurrection is firmly based upon the events of that first Easter. To try to suggest what this means for us, I quote some words of the scientist and theologian Dr John Polkinghorne:

> My understanding of the soul is that it is the almost infinitely complex, dynamic, information-bearing pattern . . . of my animated body and continuously developing . . . during the course of my earthly life. That psychosomatic unity is dissolved at death by the decay of my body, but I believe it is a perfectly coherent hope that the pattern which is me will be remembered by God and . . . will be recreated by him when he reconstitutes me in the new environment of his choosing.[14]

In simpler terms, we might say that the essential 'me' will be brought back to life beyond my death by God in a form suited to the world of eternity.

It is this hope that can give ultimate meaning to life for those facing death. But are older people (and others) given help to lives their lives 'sub specie aeternitatis' (with an eternal perspective) as Christians so evidently did in New Testament times? There is much truth in the observation that death is the taboo subject of our day. Our culture goes to great lengths to propagate the myths that we need not grow old and that even death may in due course be indefinitely delayed or even defeated by medical science. Gone are the Victorian days when the fact of death was a prime means of focusing people on the need to repent in order to inherit eternal life, or when 'the four last things' (death, judgement, heaven and hell) formed the staple diet for the Sundays in Advent! In such a climate of denial it is not surprising that many of our respondents did not warm to the suggestion that more attention might be given in church to the subject of death.

However, older people are not well-served by such a head-in-the-sand approach. Advertising for the Alpha programme, with its suggestion that simply going through the motions of living for 80 years or so is insufficient recipe for a truly fulfilling life, perhaps strikes the right note. Older people do need help in coming to terms with death and how it challenges the whole meaning and purpose of life. Anything less is surely a betrayal.

## CONTINUED SPIRITUAL GROWTH

Most Christians seek to grow in their understanding of God and in their own spiritual lives all their days. The first stated purpose of the Christian Council on Ageing, established in 1982, is: 'to explore the Christian potential and vocation in later life and nurture the continuing development of faith and growth'.

However, the assumption can too easily be made that older people will have reached a plateau in their spiritual development and are unlikely to progress much further. Kenneth Howse notes that a 1992 working party report from the dioceses of Rochester and Canterbury observed that, because of such assumptions, 'clergy were sometimes more willing to offer a careful ministry of preaching, teaching and pastoral care to young people than old'.[15]

Redressing this situation will require that churches recognise that there is a different and very special spiritual agenda that older people face.

There are certainly three areas in which such growth in faith and spirituality can be most marked and in which older people can be helped or hindered by the Church.

### Communion with God
Our own research demonstrated that prayer is a continuing and regular practice for very many older people, including those who do not go to church. Whilst a high proportion reported that they prayed with others or at Holy Communion, some 90% said that they also prayed on their

own. Such solitariness gives a predisposition towards contemplative prayer which may be seen as movement towards the final stage in James Fowler's model of spiritual development, preoccupation with Universalising Faith. Richter and Francis describe this as when 'preoccupation with the self gives way to a sense of mystical unity with all things'. [16] Unpublished research by Graham Keyes of the Simeon and Anna Project [17] seems to show how many people's perceptions of God and of prayer do change in older age, God becoming more of a presence than a person and prayer a matter of contemplation rather than petition. It also helps to explain why over a third of Richter and Francis' older church leavers identified by secondary analysis believed that God is essentially within a person and so churches are not indispensable.

This is obviously at loggerheads with the value that society at large and the Church appear to place on words rather than reflection and on doing and achieving over against being. Philosopher Harry Moody is quoted in Howse:[18] 'This failure to understand contemplation poses a grave problem in the process of growing old today. Without some feeling for the virtues of . . . inwardness, patience etc . . . it is impossible to understand what ego-transcendence in old age might ultimately be about . . . We can only form a distorted image of it and call it quietism or disengagement.'

Such lack of empathy may be the reason why some older people find it necessary to leave their church in order to have space to go on growing towards this kind of maturity. Indeed, secondary analysis of the data provided by Richter and Francis found that 28% of their older respondents felt that the Church no longer helped them to grow and rather more that a questioning faith did not seem to be acceptable. (Conversely, it needs to be said that an equivalent number were looking for greater certainty in the Church's teaching.)

They comment: 'It may be that, if churches take increasing account of people's need to grow in faith, "outgrowing" the church may one day be followed by "growing back into" the church.' [19] It could be a big 'if', especially for older people who do not have the luxury of time being on their side. One of the most powerful of the statistics produced by Richter and Francis remains that almost two thirds of all their church leavers declared that it was they who had changed, it was not the fault of the Church.[20] It is a sad commentary upon the Church's reluctance to accompany people through their life journey of continual change and growth.

## The diminishment of advancing years

Paul Tournier, quoted in Howse,[21] poses the question well: 'How can the person who has seen a meaning in life also see a meaning in old age, which seems to him to be a diminution, an amputation, a stifling of life?' Older people often suffer an accumulation of such losses and diminishments which are likely to include retirement with the consequential loss of role, moving from the family home, health problems, and, of course, bereavements.

Enabling people to see that they can 'grow' spiritually through such experiences is a very significant theological and pastoral challenge.[22] Profound theological questions are raised and sometimes it seems that older Christians are not expected or 'allowed' to doubt or question. The temptation may be to deny the importance of such questions or simply to counterbalance the losses with the acknowledgement of those things that still remain for the ageing person. There is, however, a limit to this balancing act when the former manifestly outweighs the latter.

More positively, there is the need to encourage people experiencing such diminishment to recognise how this can be a means of learning more about God and our essential dependency upon him. It is much more than fatalistic acceptance. 'Letting go' is very hard for previously active people to accept, especially when they have been schooled in 'the Protestant (or should it be British?) work ethic'. The highly active and high achieving St Paul learned from his experience of periodic and debilitating illness how reliant he was upon the grace of God and that, paradoxically, when he was weak, then he was strong – in a strength not his own. Many other saints of the spiritual life can be our teachers here.

However, the greatest inspiration of all is found in the passion of Christ, as William Vanstone has shown in his very helpful book, *The Stature of Waiting.* [23] At the heart of the Christian faith is the belief that Jesus accomplished his mightiest work, the salvation of humankind, only when his active ministry was at an end and he was 'done to' in the last stages of his life culminating in the cross. Older people facing progressive diminishment and 'being done to' can be helped to see 'letting go' as more truly 'handing over to God' so that his will may be accomplished most fully. Such a faith development contains within it the possibility of the most significant and ultimate spiritual growth of all, in Charles Wesley's words:

> Till death thy endless mercies seal,
> And make the sacrifice complete.

## Peace at the last

The spoken, or more usually unspoken, desire and prayer of many older people is that they should die 'at peace': with other people who are important to them, with themselves and their lives, and with God. Everyone carries through life with them the burden of past injuries and hurts that they have received from or inflicted upon other people. Often they have never 'made it up', so relationships are harmed, soured or broken. Sometimes such hurts may go back very many years and the other person has long since died. Survivors of the wars of the past century may have deeply traumatic memories. Family carers, who are often themselves elderly, can also harbour very troublesome guilt feelings about what they regard as their lapses and shortcomings in coping lovingly. The time for reconciliation is short and may in some cases involve the quite deep healing of memories. Such pain should never be glossed over, nor the need for healing seen as other than urgent. The story of the two criminals at Calvary leads us to believe that it is never impossible or too late.

The biblical concept of peace (or 'shalom') is, of course, much more than the absence of war and the healing of hurts. It has to do with the wholeness or integrity of a person in all their life and relationships. Such integration involves making sense of the totality of life, coming to terms with what one has and has not achieved, and finding in God the one who can make up what is lacking. This is 're-membering' not just in the sense of recalling but of pulling everything together into one whole – the opposite of the 'dis-membering' or fragmentation that can characterise so much of life. It is this process that can bring the deepest sense of fulfilment, of wholeness and of peace, and it can rightly be seen as the final item of the spiritual agenda of this life. And, of course, there always remains for Christians the hope of the 'how-much-more' that surely lies beyond this life.

Howse notes how the White House Conference on Ageing as long ago as 1961 contended that 'religion, in its teaching, ritual and organisation, is uniquely equipped to guide and aid men in making the closing years of life a time of deepening fulfilment'.[24] We need to ask whether the Church as a whole and our own local church are successful in doing this, or whether it even appears to be on its agenda.

The following questions can profitably be considered by local churches and their leaders if they want to take seriously the faith needs of older (and other) people:

1.  Are books available within the church for those troubled by the challenges in modern society to the Christian faith and the spiritual issues faced by older people? (There has been a proliferation of the latter in recent years and a select list will be found at the end of this book.)

2.  Do the study, fellowship and growth groups available in the church encourage older people to share both their doubts and their Christian experience? If not, or if there is no such opportunity, should a special Alpha (or Emmaus or Discipleship) course be arranged specially for older people and at a suitable time of day?

3.  Does the teaching input in sermons ever deal with the 'last things' of life? If not, should a short course be arranged?

4.  Do sermons constantly urge people to 'do something'? Is sufficient consideration given to those who feel that there is little they can now do?

5. Is there scope to hold a series of 'open meetings/lectures' when issues about science and religion, the nature of the Bible etc can be honestly addressed? If so, how can it be advertised to reach thinking people both within and outside the church?

6. Instead of an evangelistic mission of outreach project, should the church devote a year to a 'school for prayer', introducing people to a variety of approaches including contemplative methods?

### References

1 Peter Brierley, *The Tide is Running Out*, Christian Research, 2000, chapter 4.

2 Peter Coleman, *Stability and change in religious attitudes with ageing in a 20 years longitudinal study*, paper delivered to British Society of Gerontology Conference, September 2000.

3 Richter and Francis, op. cit. pp.18-19.

4 Bertrand Russell, *Mysticism and Logic*, Routledge, 1918, pp.47ff.

5 Keith Ward, *God, Faith and the New Millennium*, One World Publications, 1998, p.123.

6 Paul Davies, *The Mind of God*, Penguin, 1992, p.232.

7 Keith Ward, op. cit. p.217.

8 Grace Davie, *Believing Without Belonging*, Blackwell, 1994.

9 Grace Davie, 'The Institutional Churches: a non-statistical perspective', *Epworth Review*, Methodist Publishing House, April 2000, p.19ff.

10 *Finding Faith in 1994*, The Lent '94 Research Project, Churches Together in England, 1995, table 9.

11 Howse, op. cit. p.8ff.

12 Richter and Francis, op. cit. p.32.

13 Hans Küng, *Does God Exist?*, HarperCollins, 1980.

14 John Polkinghorne, *Science and Christian Belief*, SPCK, 1994, p.163.

15 Howse, op. cit. p.48.

16 Richter and Francis, op. cit. p.55.

17 Referred to by Michael Butler in *Spiritual Perspectives on Ageing*, Methodist Homes for the Aged, 1998, p.E6. Information about Simeon and Anna from: Rev Graham Keyes, 1 East Avenue, Benton, Newcastle upon Tyne NE12 9PH.

18  Howse, op. cit. p.99.
19  Richter and Francis, op. cit. p.64.
20  Ibid, p.64.
21  Howse, op. cit. p.63.
22  Ibid, p.64.
23  William Vanstone, *The Stature of Waiting*, DLT, 1982.
24  Howse, op. cit. p.60.

# CHAPTER SIX

# EVANGELISING

*I stopped going to church when I was a teenager, and didn't go back until I was middle-aged.*

*I dropped out of church when I was ten, and didn't go again for 45 years.*

*My husband didn't want me to go to church, so I never went until after he died. Now I've been going for about three years.*

These are not unusual stories. As people age they tend to have fewer choices open to them. However, one choice that some older people made in the 1990s was to start attending church, perhaps for the first time, or after a gap of many years. As previous chapters have pointed out, older people have been coming back to church in the 1990s, the only age group to do so. The following maps, reproduced by permission of Christian Research, show the percentage of those aged 65 or over who attend church, and reveal how that percentage has changed in the nine years between the English Church Census of 1989 and the English Church Attendance Survey of 1998.

## MAP 1: Percentage of Sunday churchgoers 65 or over, England, 1989

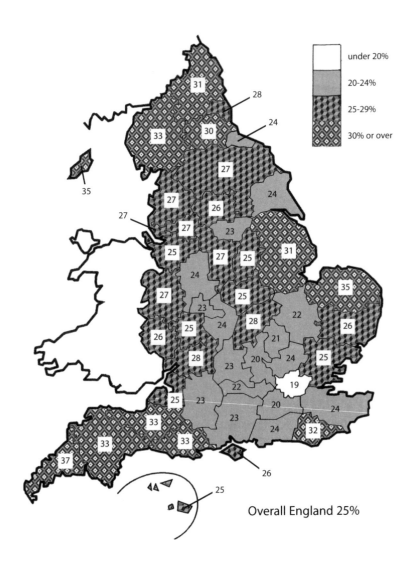

Overall England 25%

*Figure 1: Church Attendance by Age, England, 1989 & 1998*

## MAP 2: Percentage of Sunday churchgoers 65 or over, England, 1998

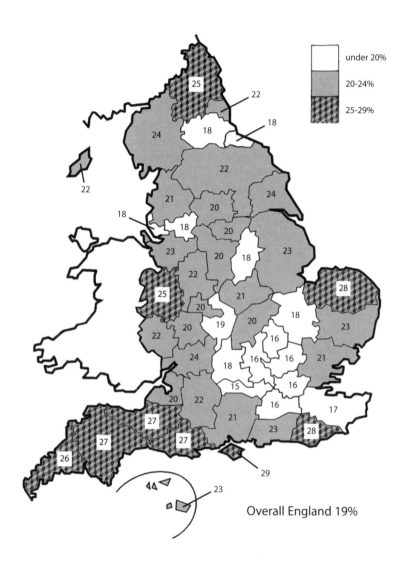

Overall England 19%

*Figure 1: Church Attendance by Age, England, 1989 & 1998*

If older people are returning to church or coming for the first time, can more be encouraged to do so? The two groups of older people on whom evangelistic efforts could usefully be focused are very different: those who have been to church at some time in their past and for whom church is part of their life story, and those who have never been. Some of those who have been regular attenders in the past have been hurt in some way and may not be at all interested in coming back to church. Others may still think of themselves as churchgoers, but they just haven't been for quite a while!

Almost half the churchgoers in the survey had stopped attending for at least a year at some time in their lives. They were now back attending regularly, but there are many others who have not yet come back and might well be open to doing so. Richter and Francis have quantified this, suggesting that three out of five people who once attended church fairly regularly no longer do so – a total of over 18 million.[1] That is a very large number of people for whom church attendance has been a part, perhaps a major part, of their life story.

For older people especially, the Christian faith is not unknown. They are much more likely than today's children to have attended Sunday school, and at day school they studied Scripture rather than Religious Education. They are, therefore, aware of the meaning of Christmas and Easter and are familiar with many of the well-known Bible stories. Christian moral values still underpin their attitudes to family and society.

Many older non-churchgoers still hold to the major tenets of the Christian faith such as belief in a personal God. The survey showed the extent of belief in five doctrines: God created the world; he is a God of love; Jesus Christ was more than just a man; Jesus Christ rose from the dead; and God can influence my life today. Between one third and two-fifths of non-churchgoers believed 'strongly' in each doctrine. While this is roughly half the level of belief of churchgoers, nevertheless there were more non-churchgoers who believed in each doctrine 'strongly' than who chose either of the other options of less certainty or definite non-belief.

The non-churchgoers in the survey were not necessarily non-Christian. For many of them it is the case that they simply do not currently attend church, at least, not regularly!

## BELONGING, FAITH AND THE PRESENCE OF GOD

Chapter three states: 'Probably the major cause of the marginalisation of older people in churches is that they have lost that sense of "belonging".' That is not only true of older people *in* churches – many of those who no longer attend dropped out because they lost a sense of belonging. Why did that happen? Many of them stopped attending church at a time of major change in their lives: when they left school, on leaving home to go away to college or to fight in the second world war, at marriage or the birth of children, or later in life when a long-loved spouse died. Interestingly, those are also some of the events that can bring people back into contact with church!

Our survey showed that many who had left church had found a sense of belonging elsewhere, often with neighbours or in a local club or society. In the focus group discussions it was clear that this had met for them the need to identify with a group of like-minded people. They saw the way churchgoers belong to church as similar, and meeting the same need. However, for many churchgoers 'belonging' goes deeper than that.

### What does belonging mean?

The way women churchgoers perceive belonging has been studied, although it is not known whether men sense belonging differently.[2] For women there are five levels of belonging which are particularly important when joining a new congregation, whether they are coming to church for the first time or looking for a new place of worship, perhaps after moving home.

*Being known.* For many women it is important that people know them by name, it helps with a sense of identity. For someone living alone, Sunday morning may be the first time they have spoken to anyone since coming home from work on Friday evening, and for widowed or divorced people conversations at church may be the only meaningful ones they have face-to-face with anyone all week.

*Being valued.* However, belonging goes deeper. It is about being valued as a person, for who you are, not only for what you do. Perhaps for older people it is being valued for what they are now, and not for what they once were. It is an awareness that others in the church are glad that you come to their church and are willing to show a personal interest in you over a period of time. This level of belonging may be reached quite quickly, for some women even on the first visit, and for others usually within a few weeks.

*Feeling accepted.* This is the next level of belonging, and is a very important stage. It is being accepted, whatever a woman's idiosyncrasies, strengths or weaknesses. Women described it in phrases such as 'I feel part of the family', 'I feel at home', 'I can be myself without being frowned at.' It takes much longer to reach this level of belonging, sometimes as much as two years. A trust has to be built up before most women are willing to expose their weaknesses, and that takes time. It was, therefore, a more significant factor for women in feeling they belonged. It was reaching the point of feeling 'on the inside' rather than still thinking of oneself as a visitor or newcomer.

*Being involved.* Women want to be involved, not just spectators at church. Whether they make coffee, teach Sunday School or join a church committee, is in one sense irrelevant. A job in the church, whatever it is, gives a sense of identity. For most of the women in the women's research this desire to be involved was strong, even if their lives were already very busy. Those who were not involved in some way, however small, felt themselves on the outside, looking in on all that happened but not really part of it. The older people's focus groups suggest it is this level of belonging which older people lose first. When they give up a role in the church, whether because they pass it on to someone younger, or because they are no longer able to do it, they suffer a kind of bereavement. The loss is not only of the job, but of the sense of involvement which is diminished, and that may lead to a gradual loss of the feeling of belonging.

*God had called her there.* For some women there was a very strong spiritual sense that they were in the right church. Not everyone wanted to use the word 'called', a term that is perhaps more frequently found among evangelicals. However, the same conviction about the rightness of worshipping in a particular church was experienced by people from many church traditions and all ages. This aspect of belonging was linked for some people to feeling a strong sense of God's presence, particularly in worship but sometimes in other contexts also.

Unpublished private surveys by Christian Research of local congregations reveal that three factors are consistently interrelated: a strong sense of belonging, a growth in faith, and sensing God's presence in worship. It is the second and third factors which make belonging to a faith community different from belonging to the local social club or feeling at home with one's neighbours. A sense of belonging in church is strongest for those who attend at least once a month. Those who go less often than they used to (which may well be true of older people as they get less mobile) are likely to report that their sense of belonging has weakened.

One way to draw older people (and others) back to church could be to seek to reawaken or refocus a desire for worship or faith. The non-churchgoers surveyed were not unaware of spiritual issues; they were not only willing but also able to answer a question about their sources of spiritual nourishment. Their top two answers, hymns and songs (57%) and *Songs of Praise* (50%), reveal a love for church music of the sort usually used in worship services. One woman, who by her own admission had not attended church regularly since she was a child, nevertheless said, 'I sometimes slip into the back of a service because I like the music. The atmosphere in church is helpful.' Was she perhaps sensing the presence of God in the 'atmosphere', without realising that's what it was?

It is increasingly being recognised that people these days often need to belong before they come to believe. A major book by Professor Robin Gill, *Churchgoing and Christian Ethics,* sets out this perspective.[3] It used to be the opposite way round:

'I believe, therefore I come to church', followed by a gradual growth into belonging there. That was the ethos behind mass evangelism such as the Billy Graham Crusades. Now it is much more likely that one of hundreds of different reasons draws a person to the church. If they find a welcome and like what goes on, they may begin to feel they belong before they reach a point of being able to say they believe.

## COMING BACK

People who have stopped attending church need a reason to come back. Finding a welcome when attending an event other than a worship service may be the encouragement they require. If it is something they can come to regularly, then over time they are likely to start feeling they belong. Eventually this may lead to them finding faith.

What kind of ways might help older folk to take the first step to come into church?

### 'Occasional Offices'

The Occasional Offices of baptism, marriage and funerals are key times of contact, especially for the established churches. Although numbers for such are dropping, there are still many families who turn to the Church to have a baby baptised, to get married, or for the funeral of a family member. Grandparents are very likely to be among the family members who come to a christening, indeed it may well be the grandparents who have encouraged the parents to seek such a service.

One of the hard things for older people is facing the death of friends and other family members of their generation. Fairly regularly they may find themselves in church for a funeral or taking part in a Christian service at a crematorium.

If those who come to such events, of whatever age, have previously attended church regularly, would it not be good if they found such a warm welcome that they recognised the possibility of belonging once again? And for those who have never been, perhaps they might discover that church is not the institutional, boring stereotype they thought it was.

Many churches have bereavement counselling and follow-up programmes in place. Although our research did indeed show that some people leave church because of bereavement, the percentage of non-churchgoers who attend *more* after a bereavement is actually greater than those who attend less.

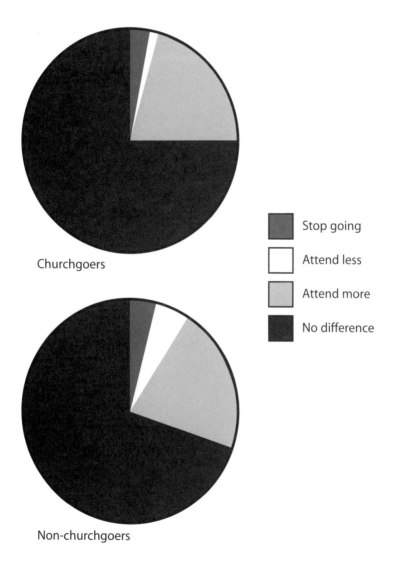

Churchgoers

Stop going

Attend less

Attend more

No difference

Non-churchgoers

*Figure 2: Impact on Church Attendance of spouse's death*

In another research project among women churchgoers,[4] one senior citizen widow said, 'The church is a place where widows are honoured and dignified in a way that is rare in society.' Grief is a painful and lonely process, but having supportive friends around is one of the most helpful ways of moving through the anger, guilt or other aspects of bereavement. To become whole again after the loss of a loved one after perhaps many years of marriage or close friendship is a difficult task. For a bereaved person it is important that they have a safe place where they can learn again to be a single person, somewhere where they are accepted and appreciated for who they are and not only for what they were. Offering such a place for those who have been bereaved can be a key means of reaching out to older people.

Among the non-churchgoers in the focus groups there was a distinct feeling that they wanted the church to be there when they need it. That, of course, puts pressure on already busy pastoral workers and ministers. But if older people are to find their way to, or back to, faith, they often need to first find their way to, or back to, the church. Being there when they need us at the key events of life can be a first step.

**Music**
It could be that for many viewers, *Songs of Praise* goes some way towards meeting the three areas outlined above: of spiritual growth, a feeling of belonging, and a sense of God's presence. The hub of the programme is, of course, the singing of Christian hymns and songs, either by the congregation, a choir, group or soloist. The majority of the hymns are ones that older people will remember from their childhood, along with some of the newer songs of which there has been such a proliferation in recent years. Television is not very good at conveying atmosphere because viewers are spectators rather than participants. However, the programme's producers do their best to help viewers feel part of the event, not only by their filming of people singing but by tastefully mixing such pictures with ones of the church building or local natural beauty.

The people who are interviewed on *Songs of Praise* are always members of the local community and, although they rarely say which church they attend, it is clear that most of them also belong to one of the congregations in the area. In the course of the interview they usually share how God has helped them in difficult or even tragic circumstances, and the strength of their faith can be a beacon of hope to viewers under similar pressure. The fact that respondents to the survey put *Songs of Praise* so high on their list of sources of spiritual nourishment suggest that it does indeed help to meet their needs for worship, belonging, or growth in faith. And the older they were, the more the programme provided spiritual nourishment.

How could churches use non-churchgoers' interest in church music to reach out to them? Here are some examples:

Songs of Praise-type services are held up and down the country. They are common during the holiday months in seaside resorts, but by no means limited to such locations. If the event is well planned (and locals realise the cameras won't be there!), they can attract a variety of people who would not normally attend.

A rural church has a programme of holding concerts and choral events, which is much appreciated by villagers. The fact that the events are nearby rather than in the nearest conurbation, and probably cheaper than a ticket for a major concert hall, are both pluses. The church has recently refurbished its buildings in order to make them more conducive to worship as well as the musical events.

An Early Music Festival in a cathedral city holds many of its events in local churches, which have a suitable atmosphere for this particular kind of music. Other music festivals regularly hold events in churches.

Such activities bring people in because of their love of the music. Once there, a contact can be established and then strengthened, so perhaps encouraging further visits for more directly 'spiritual' activities.

## Community activities

In one of the focus groups a non-churchgoer said, 'People won't come to church on Sunday, but they will come mid-week. Why don't you take the church to them?' Increasing numbers of churches are doing just that, sometimes on their own premises and sometimes in other ways.

The English Church Attendance Survey found that four churches in every nine hold some kind of mid-week activity which attracts people who do not regularly attend worship services.[5] On average such activities reached 37 adults (over 15 years of age) and 33 children per week. That works out at 2.4% of the entire population who are involved with the church in some way in a mid-week activity. These people are 'warm contacts' who may already feel they belong to that church. Befriending them and helping that sense of belonging to grow could awaken interest in faith issues as well as practical ones.

At Christian Research we regularly arrange seminars or research briefings. It is getting more and more difficult to find churches with a suitably sized hall which they are willing to rent out for such events. Many of them have so many activities going on that they can't fit us in! Church halls especially can be fully booked all week, with events such as lunch clubs, playgroups, parent and toddler groups, drop-in centres, activity clubs, keep fit, line dancing, day-time discipleship courses (such as Alpha or Emmaus). Not all of these are aimed at older people, although some are, and they would be welcome at many of the others. As suggested in chapter two parent and toddler can equal grandparent and toddler in these days when many mothers work full-time and a grandparent provides the childcare!

> A church in a deprived suburb of a provincial city did a survey of the needs in their area. They found amongst other things that there was no luncheon club for the elderly. So they started one. Other activities were offered as well as the meal, including

a monthly short worship service. After a few months they asked those who came which of the activities they liked best. The worship service was the most popular, even though hardly any of the luncheon club clients were regular churchgoers.

Church-run community activities, of course, don't only take place on church premises. Many congregations take short services in residential homes for older people. The survey did not get a good representation from such people, so this particular research project does not provide evidence of the value of such activities. Nevertheless, as earlier chapters have pointed out, they may be the sole remaining source of spiritual nourishment for many residents.

Chapter three contains many more suggestions of ways in which churches can be practically involved in the lives of older people, whether on church premises or not.

## Christian moral values

Those in the focus groups were asked what they liked about church. One of the factors that came up several times for non-churchgoers was Christian moral values. Older people are probably less likely to be affected by the changing values of postmodernity. They still believe in right and wrong, and in moral absolutes. They find it increasingly difficult to relate to young people. They don't understand advertising or why television programmes don't always seem to have a 'proper story'. They wonder what is happening to society, and many of them would like the church to speak up for what they might describe as decency.

The popularity of many training courses and the University of the Third Age shows that older people haven't necessarily stopped learning. Indeed, in a survey for the Baptist Union, *The Impact and Potential of a Greying Population on Baptist Churches in England,* completed in May 2000, Dawn Brown was surprised to find a high level of interest among older churchgoers in having a variety of learning opportunities through their church.

Could churches tap into this interest, especially of Third Age older people? Perhaps they could lay on a series of lectures or debates on moral and other issues (not necessarily on spiritual matters). Again it helps to meet a felt need for people, while also offering a way of discovering a welcome in a church.

## Prayer

Older people pray – including non-churchgoers! Eighty-five per cent of churchgoers in our survey prayed daily, but so did 65% of non-churchgoers, with only 5% saying they hardly ever prayed. What they prayed about was fairly similar, although as might be expected, churchgoers were more likely to spend time praising and worshipping God, especially those who prayed every day.

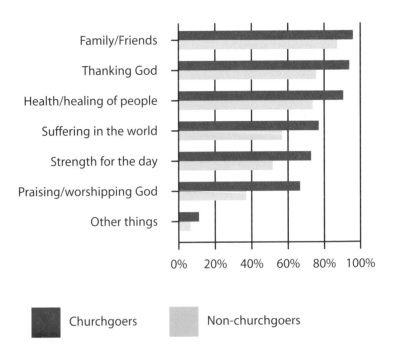

*Figure 3: What people prayed about*

If many older non-churchgoers pray regularly, can that be used as a means of evangelism?

> Members of a church in a run-down urban environment visited every home in their area. They didn't invite people to services, but simply asked if there was anything people would like them to pray about. The requests they were given were prayed for at the daily mass at the church.

> In several places the local Churches Together group has put up a box in a local supermarket, inviting people to put in prayer requests. In one scheme in south-east London the number of requests being put in the box is gradually growing. Matters for prayer are shared out among churches willing to take part.

When an unknown person rings the doorbell, residents can be forgiven for thinking it is either the Jehovah's Witnesses or somebody wanting money. Many, of course, still give generously by this means to regular events such as Christian Aid week. But it is a new idea to them to be asked if they have a need which the church could help meet or pray about!

In a garden or the countryside is where older people are most likely to experience God's presence other than in a church. There is a movement sponsored by The Quiet Garden Trust which encourages the ministry of hospitality and prayer on an occasional basis in private homes and gardens and the environs of other places such as schools, hospitals and retreat houses.[6] Perhaps small groups could use such facilities as a means of outreach to older people who are willing to explore the possibilities of prayer that they offer.

## Practicalities

As we have seen in chapter two, for many older people church buildings are impractical. They may be too cold in winter, have inaccessible toilets, or none at all. Pews are uncomfortable, and even if they have been replaced with chairs those may not be much better! With the passing of the Disability Discrimination legislation, all churches are having to face up to access issues such as the precipitous flight of steps instanced in chapter two. There has even been a case of a church being threatened with being taken to court because its services were not available in Braille. Hopefully it will not be too long before issues of access are a thing of the past, and anyone with a hearing aid can hear what is going on via a loop system! It is important that such matters are addressed so that when older people or others with disabilities wish to attend church there are not practical reasons why they cannot.

## USING THE PEOPLE WE HAVE

In *The Tide is Running Out*, Peter Brierley wrote about older people, 'How can we help these people, often with energy, health, and because of earlier retirement free time, to *use their gifts constructively* to reach out? . . . We need to encourage and enable them into mission while we still have them.'[7]

Our survey identified four groups of older people: those under retirement age but who have retired early, those aged 65 to 74 who are often referred to as in their Third Age, those aged 75 to 84 who are the active frail, and those over 85 who are the less active frail. Clearly not all older people fit neatly into these age categories – in my own church we have a man of 102 who is just beginning to move into the less active frail category!

The first two groups are a vital people resource in many churches. The survey clearly showed that many older people, especially in rural churches or churches where the congregation is made up of mostly older people, are continuing to take a very active role in the leadership and running of the church. They may be a churchwarden, treasurer, deacon or member of the PCC, still teaching in Sunday school, leading a home group, or fulfilling one of the myriad other tasks needed to keep a church functioning. Many churches might well grind to a halt if their older members retired from activity in the church at the same time as they retire from employment!

One of the things the older people in our survey wanted was for their experience to be heard and valued, and when appropriate still used.  Some of the older people in a congregation will have been involved in evangelism earlier in their Christian experience.  Rather than being left to 'get on with it' as and when they have personal opportunity, can such people be involved in the evangelism programme of the church?  Not everyone will be comfortable with that, but they could perhaps be helped to do so.  Brown's Baptist survey asked about learning opportunities provided by churches for older people, and also what learning opportunities the older people would value.  The answers tabulated below show the potential for equipping people to be involved in evangelising, both at home and overseas!

|  | Church offers training % | Would like training % |
|---|---|---|
| Sharing your faith with others of the same age | 36 | 34 |
| Sharing your faith with other age groups | 29 | 37 |
| Overseas missionary training and opportunities | 12 | 7 |

*Table 1: Training opportunities for older people*

Other areas of training asked about by the respondents in Brown's survey were Information Technology, issues relating to bereavement, retirement etc, and help with personal spiritual development – something 40% of them would like.

Training does not necessarily have to take place in a formal training course.

A minister in a seaside retirement town wanted to visit all the homes in the area.  He could not do this alone and asked for volunteers from the congregation, most of whom were themselves retired.  Initially nobody was willing to help.  He persuaded one person to join him, and for three months they went visiting together.  At the end of that time both the minister and the other person took someone else with them, again for three months and so on. After a couple of years the majority of the congregation were taking part in the visiting programme, including people who previously would have run a mile from such involvement.

Like anyone else in churches older people are not limited to reaching out to their own age group. They often have a particular opportunity in relation to their grandchildren. In a private survey by Christian Research of why children aged 10 to 14 leave the Church of Scotland, one of the questions asked was why children of that age attend. The range of possible answers included 'Parents bring them'. There was the option of adding other answers and one offered by several respondents was 'Grandparents bring them'.

For single parent families or ones in which both parents work, grandparents are often an important source of childcare, either before children are old enough to go to school or, when they are older, before and after school hours. Perhaps one of the ways forward for helping children find faith is to help their grandparents to share it with them.

A church in an area with many retired people became very concerned about how few of the children who did live in the area actually attended church. They responded to their concern by putting on a short course for grandparents on how to share their faith with their grandchildren.

There is a danger that churches whose congregations are mainly elderly settle into a kind of siege mentality. One respondent to the 1989 English Church Census, when asked about the future prospects for growth of the church, replied that they were all over 80 and 'just waiting to die'. The corollary, of course, is that it is not only the individual members who die, but sometimes the church itself. Perhaps that particular group of people were now too frail to seek fresh vision for themselves and their church.

## CONCLUSION

Quite a number of those in the focus groups shared the vision of their church, and wanted to be part of seeing it fulfilled. Their expectation was that the leaders of the church should clarify and direct that vision. If they were happy with the leadership of their church – and unfortunately not all were – they were mostly willing to follow the vision set out by those leaders.

Evangelising older people, therefore, has two aspects. Much of this book has focused on programmes and events which appeal to older people and which may draw them into the church and into a deeper faith commitment. However, there is also the dimension of encouraging and helping those already in the church to catch the vision to reach out to others and to get involved as far as they are able. Evangelism, whether of older people or of those of any age, cannot be left entirely to the clergy. Lay involvement is an increasingly important aspect of church life in all denominations as a decreasing number of clergy face ever-growing demands. Many older people in their Third Age and perhaps beyond would welcome a fresh challenge and new vision, provided they are offered realistic ways of being involved. For some, that could well be in evangelism.

---

**References**
1  Richter and Francis, op. cit. p.xii.
2  Heather Wraight, *Eve's Glue*, Christian Research to be published 2001.
3  Robin Gill, *Churchgoing and Christian Ethics*, CUP 1999.
4  Wraight op. cit.
5  Peter Brierley, *The Tide is Running Out*, Christian Research, 2000, chapter 7.
6  The Quiet Garden Trust, Stoke Oak Farm, Park Road, Stoke Poges, Slough SL2 4PG.
7  Brierley op. cit. p.235.

# Appendix 1

# 40 QUESTIONS AND SUGGESTIONS FOR CHURCHES
## based on the chapters of this book

1.  What percentage of our congregation / church membership are over 65 / over 85?

2.  Hold a focus group for older people using the framework suggested in Appendix 4.

3.  Consider using the questionnaire in Appendix 5, or an abbreviated version, with the older people in the church and local community?

4.  What priority is given to older people in our mission statement / strategy?

5.  What priority does our minister / ministry team give to working with older people?

6.  How many people over 65 occupy leadership positions in the church, and for how long have they held office?

7.  Carry out an audit of the premises, with the involvement of older people, to find out how friendly they are towards those who are frail or disabled.

8.  Do we have an effective transport policy for getting older people to church services and other events?

9.  Do we have a 'welcome rota' at church and how effective is it?

10. What is our practice for commending people who move to a church in their new area?

11. Do we maximise the opportunities presented by festivals like Christmas and Easter to contact everyone in the community?

12. Is there the need for a lunch club for older people in our community?

13. Is there a policy to take pastoral care and worship into local care homes?

14. Do we know of those in our congregation (of whatever age) who have recently experienced major life events such as retirement, marital breakdown, significant bereavement, hospitalisation or needing to care for family members at home? Do we offer appropriate support?

15. How many people in the congregation / local community are caring for people with dementia in the family or amongst friends?

16. Would someone with dementia feel welcome at our church services and other gatherings?

17. How many of our older members are *not* actively involved in any fellowship group?

18. What opportunities for intergenerational meeting and sharing do we offer?

19. What part do older men play in our church?

20. What contribution do older people make to evangelism and mission?

21. Do older people from outside the congregation come onto church premises during the week?

22. Would a regular mid-week service be appropriate in our situation?

23. What place is there for fellowship meals in our programme?

24. What are the main social, economic and political issues faced by older people and are these taken up by the church?

25. Is the pastoral care system effective in looking after frail older people or is it mostly left to the minister?

26. Review the liturgical changes in the church over the past 20 years and consider how they have been received by older members.

27. What can we learn from the enormous popularity of *Songs of Praise* with older people?

28. How do individual older people contribute to worship in our church?

29. Do we promote 'all-age worship' and if so does it truly give due place to older people (amongst others)?

30. How effectively is Holy Communion and other worship taken to housebound older people?

31. Is our church conducive to a quiet sense of the presence of God?

32. Ask a small number of older people in the congregation to monitor services and sermons over a period of a few weeks, noting what they have found most / least helpful and relevant.

33. How do older people feature in the prayer life of the church?

34. Gather a group of older church members to discuss such subjects as: their purpose in life; what they find the greatest hindrances to faith; whether Christianity is unique; what parts of the Bible speak to them most; how confident they are of life after death; how their

idea of God has changed over the years; what further spiritual growth they seek.

35. What ministry do we exercise towards the terminally ill so that they may die in peace?

36. Is there a church library or bookstall, and if so how well does it cater for older Christians?

37. How easy is it for occasional churchgoers to follow our services?

38. Can we find a way of inviting and responding to requests for prayer from people in the wider community?

39. Is it possible to create a prayerful quiet place in the gardens or environs of the church?

40. Can we sponsor a grandparenting course?

# Appendix 2

# HALLEY STEWART AGE AWARENESS PROJECT INTERVIEW QUESTIONS

**Name:**

**Address:**

**Age group:**  65-69  70-74  75-79  80-84
              85-89  90-94  95-99

## A   RESIDENCE

1. How long have you lived here?

2. Where did you live before?

3. What family and friends do you have nearby?

4. Do you live alone?

5. If so, have you always lived alone (or for a very long time)?

6. How do you find living on your own?

**Need to note:  Any change from own home/to residential etc.  Or if recently bereaved, or long term bereaved or single.  Are there any family or friends nearby, relationships, loneliness.**

## B   GENERAL WELL-BEING

1. How well would you say that you are?

2. How do you find growing older?

3. How far would you say that you are content with life?

4. How far are you able to get out and about?

5. What daily, weekly contact do you have with other people?

**Need to note:  Satisfaction or dissatisfaction.  General health.  Human contact/loneliness.**

## C   CHURCH ATTENDANCE OR NOT

1. Have you ever belonged to the Church, now or in the past?
   a) If yes now, where?
   b) Are you able to get there?
   c) What do you enjoy about the services?
   d) Are there things that you miss compared with times past (eg the old music and traditions etc)?
   e) How well cared for by the church do you feel?

2. If you went in the distant past:
   a) Where did you go?
   b) What did you enjoy about it?
   c) What did you find helpful?
   d) How long did you go for?
   e) Why did you leave/stop going?
   f) Is there anything you miss about not going any more?
   g) Is there anything else you have put in its place?
   h) Do you ever go to church now (and in what circumstances)?

## D  FAITH AND PRAYER

1.  In what ways is your faith in older age stronger than when you were a youngster?

2.  How does your faith help you?

3.  Do you pray?

4.  When and where and how do you pray?

5.  In what ways do you find prayer beneficial/helpful?


## E  DEATH AND DYING, THE LAST THINGS

1.  Do you ever think about death?

2.  If yes, your own or another person's?

3.  What do you think about it?

4.  If no, is this something you would rather not think about?

5.  Does your own faith help you when you think about death?

6.  If so, in what ways?

7.  Do you think the Church teaches enough about life after death and judgement?

8.  What do you think about these matters?


**Need to note: It is important not to leave the person immersed in dark thoughts, so be sensitive. Remember too that this may be the first opportunity they have had to talk about these deep issues.**

## F   PRESENT OFFER

1.   As an older person, what do you feel you have to offer to the world/family/neighbourhood/church now? (Apart from helping us with our survey!)

2.   Do you feel valued?

3.   If so, by whom and how?


**Finally:**

**Stress our thanks and value them for participating and sharing.**

**Do they wish to have a copy of the report we produce in due course?**

**Make sure they know that they can contact you after the interview if anything else occurs to them upon further reflection.**

# Appendix 3

# CHRISTIAN RESEARCH QUESTIONNAIRE

(Completed prior to attendance at Focus Groups)

1. Which of these phrases best describes your lifestyle and involvement with the Church?

   ☐ I am a committed Christian and a regular attender at church

   ☐ I am a committed Christian but do not always manage to go to church as I would like

   ☐ I and my family are Christian but only go to church occasionally

   ☐ I and my family are Christian but will only go to church at Christmas or Easter

   ☐ I and my family are Christian but only go to church for occasions like weddings and funerals

   ☐ I and my family are Christian, we do not necessarily go to church but Christian ethics and morals are important to us

   ☐ I am not a Christian but an agnostic or a member of a non-Christian religion

2. If you do attend a church, which denomination do you attend?

   ☐ Anglican          ☐ URC              ☐ Independent Evangelical

   ☐ Roman Catholic    ☐ Methodist        ☐ House Church

   ☐ Baptist           ☐ Pentecostal      ☐ Congregational

   ☐ Orthodox          ☐ Other (specify) ...........................

3a. If you do not attend a church now, have you ever attended regularly?

☐ Yes    ☐ No

3b. If yes, approximately how old were you when you attended?

.......................................................................................................................

3c. If yes, which denomination did you attend?

.......................................................................................................................

3d. If yes, what was your main reason for not continuing to attend?

.......................................................................................................................

4. If you are now, or have once been involved in a church, what two things do/did you like best about it?

1. ...............................................................................................................

2. ...............................................................................................................

5. If you are now, or have once been involved in a church, what two things do/did you like least about it?

1. ...............................................................................................................

2. ...............................................................................................................

6. If you could change one thing about the Church in this country, what would you do?

.......................................................................................................................

.......................................................................................................................

Christian Research (Questionnaire)

7.  Do you ever talk about God to your neighbours, friends or people outside your own family?

    ☐ Yes    ☐ No

8.  Do you belong to any of the following clubs/organisations? (tick all that apply)

    ☐ Women's Institute    ☐ Coffee Morning

    ☐ Sports/Leisure Club    ☐ Luncheon Club

    ☐ Mothers' Union    ☐ Amateur dramatics

    ☐ Men's Club    ☐ National Trust

    ☐ Other (please specify) ............................................

9.  Which gender are you?

    ☐ Male    ☐ Female

10. Please could you indicate to which of the following age groups you belong

    ☐ 60 to 64    ☐ 70 to 74    ☐ 80+

    ☐ 65 to 90    ☐ 75 to 79

11. What is your marital status?

    ☐ Single    ☐ Widowed    ☐ Other

    ☐ Married    ☐ Divorced

Thank you for your help.

Name    ............................................................................

Address    ............................................................................

    ............................................................................

**Reproduced by kind permission of Christian Research**

# Appendix 4

# CHRISTIAN RESEARCH
## (Framework for discussion at Focus Groups)

### Introductory Questions

Do you currently go to church?

If so how frequently and which denomination?

If you still go to church, have you ever stopped going?

At what age did you stop going and how long for?

If you don't go to church now, have you ever been to church?

### Positive views of Church for Attenders and reasons for Non-Attendance

Those of you who do still go to church, what is your main reason for going?

If you've stopped going to church, why did you stop?

If you've never been, can you tell me why?

*Worship:* (appropriate sermons; known hymns; meaningful prayers; presence of God). Those of you who do go to church, which of these are true for you as to the reasons why you go?

*Worship:* (inappropriate sermons; unknown hymns; meaningless prayers; not interested in God). For those of you who do not go to church, which of these reasons are part of why you don't attend?

*Service:* (want to help others; work with a minister; use my gifts; like where the church is going). Those of you who do go to church, which of these are true for you as to the reasons why you go?

*Service:* (church people don't help others; I don't like ministers; I can use my gifts elsewhere; The church is out of touch). For those of you who do not go to church, which of these reasons are part of why you don't attend, or stopped attending?

*Practical:* (church is close by; it's of my denomination; transport is available; I'm able to both hear and see). For those of you who do go to church, which of these are true for you as to the reasons why you go?

*Practical:* (there isn't one of my denomination; I can't travel there easily; there is no wheelchair access; I can't hear and/or see). For those of you who do not go to church, which of these reasons are part of why you don't attend?

*Vision:* (share the vision; trust the leaders; like the atmosphere; this church has a future). Those of you who do go to church, which of these are true for you as to the reasons why you go?

*Vision:* (I cannot grasp the vision; I don't trust the leaders; dislike the atmosphere; I can see no future in the church). For those of you who do not go to church, which of these reasons are part of why you don't attend?

*Fellowship:* (need to belong; my friends are in the church; I meet people of other ages; there is good support in my group). Those of you who do go to church, which of these are true for you as to the reasons why you go?

*Fellowship:* (I do not feel I need to belong; I don't know anyone in the church; I can meet people of other ages elsewhere; I have other support networks). For those of you who do not go to church, which of these reasons are part of why you don't attend?

*Worth:* (perhaps half the congregation know my name; people phone if I am not there; I have lunch or tea with others occasionally; I have friends in other generations). Those of you who do go to church, which of these are true for you as to the reasons why you go?

*Worth:* (the congregation don't want to know my name; people in the church do not care; I never have lunch or tea with others; I have no friends in other generations). For those of you who do not go to church, which of these reasons are part of why you don't attend?

Other reasons for those who go to church

Other reasons for those who do not go to church

What are the most important needs that you feel are being met by going to church?

For those who don't go to church now, what needs do you think going might fulfil?

'At church I am accepted for what I am, not for what I do.' How far do you agree with this?

Would you like it to be true?

How far is it true for you?

How far is it true generally in your church?

## Negative views of Church, for Non-Attenders and Attenders

What might make you stop?

*Perception:* (church is boring; church is irrelevant; I don't need church; religion causes problems; church is only for the weak). For those of you who do not go to church, which of these reasons are part of why you don't attend?

Those of you who do go to church, which of these are true for you even though you still go?

*Practical:* (I find living out the message hard; the church is too far away; the time is inconvenient; I don't like the leadership). For those of you who do not go to church, which of these reasons are part of why you don't attend?

Those of you who do go to church, which of these are true for you even though you still go?

*Damage:* (my children wouldn't go; death of a friend/relative; own suffering/illness; husband/wife not interested). For those of you who do not go to church, which of these reasons are part of why you don't attend?

Those of you who do go to church, which of these are true for you even though you still go?

Other negative reasons for those who go to church

## Changes within the Church

In what ways do you think the experience of going to church might be different for older people than for younger people?

If you had to move what would be the characteristics you would look for in your local church?

If you wanted to go back to church what characteristics would help persuade you to do so?
If you could make one change in your local church to encourage older people more, what would it be?

**Reproduced by kind permission of Christian Research**

# Appendix 5

# HALLEY STEWART PROJECT QUESTIONNAIRE

This questionnaire will help us to find out about the needs of older people in relation to the Church. Unless otherwise stated, please tick the box next to the category that best describes your opinion.

**Part One: About You**

1. Are you

   ☐ Male  ☐ Female

2. What is your age?

   ☐ Under 60  ☐ 70 to 74  ☐ 85 to 89

   ☐ 60 to 64  ☐ 75 to 79  ☐ 90 or over

   ☐ 65 to 69  ☐ 80 to 84

3. What is your marital status?

   ☐ Single  ☐ Widowed  ☐ Other (please specify)

   ☐ Married  ☐ Divorced

**Part Two: About Church**

4. Do you currently attend church?

   ☐ Yes, at least once a month (Go to Q5a)

   ☐ Yes, between one and ten times a year (Go to Q5a)

   ☐ Not regularly, only for weddings, funerals etc (Go to Q7)

*continued . . .*

*4. continued . . .*

☐ No, but I used to (Go to Q5a)

☐ No, I've never gone regularly (Go to Q7)

5a. If at any time in your life you have stopped going to church for at least a year, at what age did you stop? (If never stopped, go to Q6)

☐ Under 20    ☐ 40 to 49    ☐ 70 to 79

☐ 20 to 29    ☐ 50 to 59    ☐ 80 or over

☐ 30 to 39    ☐ 60 to 69

5b. For how long did you stop?

☐ 1 to 5 years    ☐ 16 to 20 years

☐ 6 to 10 years    ☐ more than 20 years

☐ 11 to 15 years

5c. Why did you stop? (Tick all that apply)

☐ Family responsibilities    ☐ Because of illness

☐ Left home to study/for a job    ☐ Too far to travel

☐ Moved house    ☐ Loss of faith

☐ Moved into present accommodation

☐ Lack of time

☐ Death of a spouse

☐ Death of someone else close to me

☐ Fell out with ministers/leaders

☐ Disillusioned with the church

☐ No particular reason

☐ Other reason (please specify) _____

**Please go to Question 6**

6. Did the death of your spouse affect your churchgoing?

☐ This question does not apply

☐ Yes, I started attending more

☐ Yes, I started attending less

☐ Yes, I stopped going

☐ No, it made no difference

## Part Three: About Belonging

7. Where do you find the strongest sense of belonging, apart from family/close friends?

☐ Local club/group/activity ☐ Pub

☐ Day/Community Centre ☐ Church

☐ Among neighbours ☐ Other reason (please specify)

_____

8. How would you describe this sense of belonging?

☐ A strong sense of belonging, which is growing

☐ A strong sense of belonging, which is unchanging

☐ Strong, but not as strong as in the past

☐ I wish it was stronger

☐ I am happy to stay on the fringe

☐ Don't know

9.  Where do you have the deepest sense of God's closeness?
    (Tick all that apply)

    ☐ Outdoors, e.g. in the garden or countryside

    ☐ Whilst listening to music

    ☐ In church services

    ☐ With other people

    ☐ Other (please specify) _____

10. How often do you sense God's presence?

    ☐ Always  ☐ Occasionally  ☐ Should not expect to

    ☐ Regularly  ☐ Hardly ever  ☐ Never

**Part Four: About Your Beliefs**

11. Do you believe in a God who created the world?

    ☐ Believe strongly

    ☐ Believe most of the time

    ☐ Believe, but not sure I understand

    ☐ I'm not sure if I do believe this

    ☐ I definitely don't believe

12. Do you believe in a God of love?

    ☐ Believe strongly

    ☐ Believe most of the time

    ☐ Believe, but not sure I understand

    ☐ I'm not sure if I do believe this

    ☐ I definitely don't believe

13. Do you believe that Jesus Christ was more than just a man?

☐ Believe strongly

☐ Believe most of the time

☐ Believe, but not sure I understand

☐ I'm not sure if I do believe this

☐ I definitely don't believe

14. Do you believe that Jesus Christ rose from the dead?

☐ Believe strongly

☐ Believe most of the time

☐ Believe, but not sure I understand

☐ I'm not sure if I do believe this

☐ I definitely don't believe

15. Do you believe that God can influence your life today?

☐ Believe strongly

☐ Believe most of the time

☐ Believe, but not sure I understand

☐ I'm not sure if I do believe this

☐ I definitely don't believe

16a. Do you believe that the Church has a place of relevance in today's society?

☐ Yes     ☐ No

16b. Why do you feel this way?

_____

## Part Five:  Prayer

17a. Do you ever pray?  (If no, go to question 21)

☐ Yes          ☐ No

17b. If yes, how often do you pray?

☐ Daily                    ☐ Only in Church

☐ Weekly                   ☐ Two or three times a year

☐ Monthly                  ☐ Hardly ever

18.  How do you pray? (Tick all that apply)

☐ Alone                    ☐ Using a prayer book

☐ With others              ☐ With a minister

☐ At Communion             ☐ In my heart following a set pattern/diary/system

19.  What do you pray about? (Tick all that apply)

☐ Family/friends

☐ Things to thank God for

☐ Health/healing of particular people

☐ Suffering in the wider world

☐ Strength for the day

☐ Praising and worshipping God

☐ Other (please specify)

_____

20. Do you ever use the Lord's Prayer when you pray on your own?

☐ Yes          ☐ No

21a. As an older person, do you personally feel valued by the Church?

☐ Yes          ☐ No

21b. If yes, what makes you feel this way?

_____

21c. If no, what do you feel is the reason for this?

_____

22a. Do you feel that the Church makes good use of older people's spiritual gifts and natural talents?

☐ Yes          ☐ No

22b. If yes, are *your* spiritual gifts and natural talents used?

☐ Yes, regularly          ☐ No, but I wish they were

☐ Yes, occasionally          ☐ No, but I am happy about it

☐ Yes, they used to be in the past

**Part Seven: Getting Help**

23. Where do you find spiritual nourishment? (Tick all that apply)

☐ Books

☐ Hymns /songs

☐ Through prayer/meditation

☐ Listening to the Daily Service

*continued . . .*

143

*23. continued . . .*

☐ The Bible

☐ Church services

☐ Other church groups

☐ Through relationships

☐ Watching *Songs of Praise*

☐ Other (please specify)

_____

24. Do you watch *Songs of Praise* on BBC 1 on Sunday evening?

☐ Yes, regularly          ☐ I used to

☐ Yes, occasionally      ☐ No, not at all

25. How important is fellowship/meeting with other Christians to you?

☐ Very important          ☐ Not very important

☐ Quite important        ☐ Not important at all

☐ Important

26. Does the Church meet any of your non-spiritual needs?

☐ Yes, regularly          ☐ No, but I wish it did

☐ Yes, occasionally      ☐ No, but I am happy about it

27a. Does the Church cater physically for older people adequately?

☐ Yes          ☐ No

27b. If no what one improvement could the Church make to
improve matters?

_____

28. If you could make just one change in your local church to
encourage older people more, what would it be?

_____

**Reproduced by kind permission of Christian Research**

# Appendix 6
# SUGGESTIONS FOR FURTHER READING

*Ageing*, Church House Publications 1990

Anke, Sister *The Creativity of Diminishment*, Fairacres Publication 109

Burton-Jones, Julia *Caring for Carers*, Scripture Union 1992

Butler, Michael and Orbach, Ann *Being Your Age*, SPCK 1993

Creber, Arthur *Evangelism Among Older People*, CPAS 1995

Davis, Robert *My Journey Into Alzheimer's Disease*, Scripture Press 1993

Fischer, Kathleen *Moving On*, SPCK 1996

Guenther, Margaret *Toward Holy Ground*, DLT 1996

Jewell, Albert (ed) *Spirituality and Ageing*, Jessica Kingsley 1998

Jewell, Albert *Grow Old Along with Me*, NCEC 2001

King, Joan *Mind the Gap* (on grandparenting), NCEC 1998

Phillipson, Prue *Lesson of Love* (on Alzheimer's), Methodist Publishing House 2000

Simkins, Joan *Leading Services in Residential Homes*, Methodist Publishing House 1996

Taylor, Rhena *Love in the Shadows* (on Alzheimer's), Scripture Union 1996

Tournier, Paul *Learning to Grow Old*, Westminster/John Knox 1985

Treetops, Jackie, *A Daisy Among the Dandelions*, Faith in Elderly People, Leeds 1992

Treetops, Jackie, *Holy, Holy, Holy*, Faith in Elderly People, Leeds 1996

Vanstone, William, *The Stature of Waiting*, DLT 1982

**Relevant Grove Booklets**
18 Christians in Retirement
43 New Approaches to Ministry with Older People
81 Ageing – A Kind of Ghetto-land

## Published by Christian Council on Ageing (CCOA):

*Occasional Publications:*
- 4 The Spirituality of Ageing
- 5 Dementia – A Christian Perspective
- 6 Vocation to Retirement
- 9 Light of Faith
- 10 The Great Pilgrimage of Discovery
- 11 Dementia, Ethics and the Glory of God
- 12 What Next? Four Last Things

*Good Practice Series:*
- 2 Worship in Residential Care
- 3 Visiting Older People
- 5 Residential Care: A Christian Perspective

## Published by Methodist Homes:

Spiritual Perspectives on Ageing
*Halley Stewart Booklets:*
- 1 Spirituality in the Later Years of Life
- 2 Adapting our Lifestyle in Retirement
- 3 The Ageing Single Person
- 4 Ageing in a Strange Land
- 5 Facing Terminal Illness
- 6 Older People and Bereavement
- 7 The Spiritual Needs of People with Dementia
- 8 A Future Home
- 9 Those who Care for Others
- 10 The Church's Ministry to Ageing People

## CCOA and Methodist Homes publications can be obtained from:

The Senior Chaplain, Methodist Homes, Epworth House, Stuart Street, Derby DE1 2EQ (Tel 01332 296200)

# AUTHORS' BIOGRAPHIES

**Raymond Clarke**, a member of the United Reformed Church and former convenor of its Church and Society Department, has been Chair of Age Concern Greater London and chaired the group which produced the 1990 report *Ageing* for the Church of England Board of Social Responsibility.

**Gaynor Hammond**, a Baptist, is Dementia Project Worker with Faith in Elderly People Leeds and Yorkshire Field Worker for Northern Baptist College. She is co-writer with Laraine Moffitt of *Spiritual Care – Guidelines for Care Plans* (Christian Council Ageing and Faith in Elderly People Leeds).

**Jeffrey Harris**, a retired Methodist minister and former Secretary in the Home Mission Division of the Methodist Church, is a contributor to *Spirituality and Ageing* (Jessica Kingsley 1999), the Halley Stewart Age Awareness booklets and author of *The Great Journey of Discovery* (Christian Council of Ageing).

**Albert Jewell**, Senior Chaplain of Methodist Homes for the Aged, edited *Spirituality and Ageing* and has written *Grow Old along with Me* (NCEC 2001).

**Laraine Moffitt**, a Roman Catholic, was until the end of 2000 Worker with the Christian Council on Ageing Dementia Project in Newcastle upon Tyne, and has written the Halley Stewart booklet *The Spiritual Needs of People with Dementia.*

**Jackie Treetops**, an Anglican priest, contributed to *Spirituality and Ageing* and is author of *A Daisy among the Dandelions* and *Holy, Holy, Holy* concerning the Church's ministry with older people.

**Heather Wraight** has always been interested in what makes people tick. After training as a nurse and midwife she spent 20 years making general interest radio programmes from a Christian perspective. Now Deputy Director of Christian Research, she undertakes many of their research focus groups and interviews.